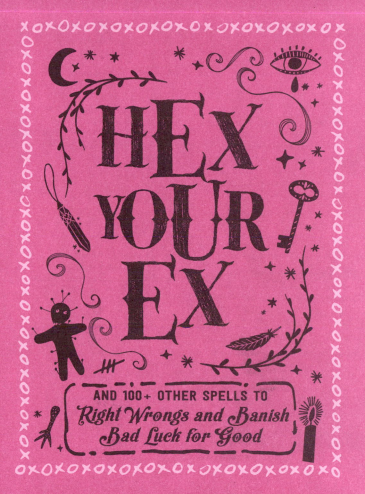

HEX YOUR EX

AND 100+ OTHER SPELLS TO

Right Wrongs and Banish
Bad Luck for Good

ADAMS MEDIA

NEW YORK   LONDON   TORONTO   SYDNEY   NEW DELHI

Adams Media
An Imprint of Simon & Schuster, Inc.
100 Technology Center Drive
Stoughton, MA 02072

Copyright © 2019 by Simon & Schuster, Inc.

All rights reserved, including the right to reproduce this book or portions thereof in any form whatsoever. For information address Adams Media Subsidiary Rights Department, 1230 Avenue of the Americas, New York, NY 10020.

First Adams Media hardcover edition January 2019

ADAMS MEDIA and colophon are trademarks of Simon & Schuster.

For information about special discounts for bulk purchases, please contact Simon & Schuster Special Sales at 1-866-506-1949 or business@simonandschuster.com.

The Simon & Schuster Speakers Bureau can bring authors to your live event. For more information or to book an event contact the Simon & Schuster Speakers Bureau at 1-866-248-3049 or visit our website at www.simonspeakers.com.

Interior design by Colleen Cunningham
Interior images © Getty Images/Utro_na_more/Nadydy

Manufactured in the United States of America

5 2022

Library of Congress Cataloging-in-Publication Data has been applied for.

ISBN 978-1-5072-0996-7
ISBN 978-1-5072-0997-4 (ebook)

Many of the designations used by manufacturers and sellers to distinguish their products are claimed as trademarks. Where those designations appear in this book and Simon & Schuster, Inc., was aware of a trademark claim, the designations have been printed with initial capital letters.

Contains material adapted from the following title published by Adams Media, an Imprint of Simon & Schuster, Inc.: *Good Spells for Bad Days* by Skye Alexander, copyright © 2009, ISBN 978-1-60550-131-4.

Readers are urged to take all appropriate precautions before attempting to cast any of the spells detailed in this book. Always follow safety and commonsense protocols while using tools or utensils, handling uncooked food, and in using matches, lighters, or any source of open flame. Please read and follow instructions and safety warnings for all tools and materials that may be employed in the spells. Although every effort has been made to provide the best possible information in this book, neither the publisher nor the author is responsible for accidents, injuries, or damage incurred as a result of tasks undertaken by readers.

Contents

Introduction

Leave bad relationships behind. Stop backstabbers in their tracks. Beat out the competition. Reclaim your personal energy. Your secret weapon? Magick!

Magick gives you the power to make the changes you need to be your best self and live the life you've always dreamed… or at least make things a little more tolerable. Frustrated by an annoying coworker at an otherwise perfect job? Use essential oils and crystal healing to improve her attitude. Worried about seeing your crazy relatives at the holidays? Whip up a protection spell that not only looks awesome, but may just give you the strength you need not to scream when your grandmother asks why you don't have a boyfriend (for the third time in a row). Is your new relationship a bit of a snooze? You guessed it—there's a spell for that too. Just ask your partner to join you in sharing a love potion to get things going.

This book will give you all the tools you need to make these—and many more!—dreams, desires, and goals come true. And why not? You deserve it! Learn to time your spells for greatest impact, discover different types of magick, and even get a few guidelines to makes sure everything goes as planned.

But remember: while these spells are designed to help you change situations in your favor, you're not practicing black magick here. No one is going to be hurt by your spellcasting. In fact, all of these (and all really worthwhile) spells are meant to empower you and give you a boost whenever you need it. You're not knocking others down...just giving yourself a little hidden advantage to make sure things work out in your favor.

So whether you want to get rid of someone who just won't take no for an answer, kick ass at work, or even just find a parking spot that doesn't completely suck, you'll find simple spells that are safe, inexpensive, and totally manageable. With more than one hundred spells for everything from cooling off an overly flirtatious friend to helping with an unexpected expense, you're sure to find the perfect spell for what you need.

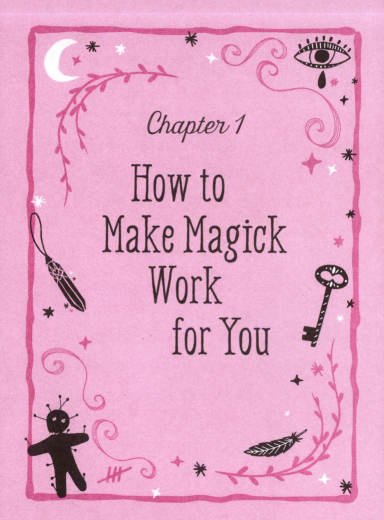

Chapter 1

How to Make Magick Work for You

No matter how much we plan, things tend to go south every once in a while: a pickpocket lifts your wallet on the subway; you accidentally hurt your friend's feelings; you catch your partner flirting with someone else. These things happen when you least expect it, through no fault of your own. But you *can* take charge of how you react to those situations...and take steps to help prevent or change them. The solution?

Magick!

Maybe you're skeptical. If you didn't believe (at least a little!), you wouldn't be here, reading this book. Maybe you're ready to get to know the world of magick and don't know where to start. You're in the right place. Or maybe you're just wondering, what's this magick stuff all about anyway? And more important, can it really help me? The answer is yes.

WHAT IS MAGICK, ANYWAY?

Magick is the act of consciously creating circumstances using methods that defy scientific logic. Whenever you form an objective in your mind, then fuel it with willpower, you're doing magick. You may not realize it yet, but you're already a practitioner! You've already done lots of spells without even knowing it. Now you're going to learn how to cast spells purposefully, to turn your luck around. All it takes is desire, a little training, and practice. Once you discover the secret, you'll be able to write your own destiny.

Once you've mastered a few basic techniques, you'll be able to cast spells for just about anything. In the following chapters, you'll find guidelines for all kinds of conjuring, plus more than one hundred good spells to fix (or, even better, prevent!) everyday mistakes and mishaps.

FOCUS YOUR WILLPOWER

The most important ingredient in any spell isn't the words or the location or even the materials you use—it's your will. When you do magick, you literally will something into being. Willpower is the energy that generates results—without it, a spell just sits there.

In magickal terms, "will" is a combination of intention, desire, and focus, and your spell's success depends on all three factors. In order for your spell to be successful, you must have a very clear picture of what you wish to accomplish; you must be passionate about achieving that objective; and you must direct energy toward the goal until you succeed. So, before you begin a spell, you should ask yourself three questions: Is your intention clear? Do you really, really want it? Can you stay focused on your goal? If you're fuzzy about what you really want, the outcome will be muddled or unsatisfactory. If you aren't passionate about your intention, you'll get lukewarm results. If you let your focus wander, it will take a lot longer to reach your goal.

In essence, here's what happens when you perform magick. Everything in the universe is composed of energy, including you. When energy particles interact, a reaction occurs. Quantum physics has demonstrated that if an observer focuses attention on energy particles, it affects their movement. When you do a magick spell, your energy influences the energy around you; your will directs the reaction to manifest the result you desire.

BELIEVE IN YOUR SPELLS...AND YOURSELF

The second most important part of spellworking is believing in yourself and your own power. If a witch doesn't believe a spell will work, it probably won't. Doubt can ruin a perfectly executed spell faster than mosquitoes can ruin a cookout. But if you have confidence in yourself and your ability to achieve your goals, anything is possible.

As you grow more adept at doing magick, your thoughts will gain power. Your intentions will materialize more quickly and accurately, so it will become increasingly important to control your thoughts and your beliefs. A witch never puts her mind on something she doesn't want to materialize. Any time you catch doubt creeping in the back door of your consciousness, stop yourself, cross out the negative thought, and replace it with a positive one.

SO WHAT KIND OF MAGICK WORKS FOR ME?

Witches and wizards, shamans and sorcerers. Whose magick is best? In the world of magick, nobody has the market cornered. If done properly, all magick works. It all stems from the same source and operates according to the same principles. Only the tools and methods differ.

For instance, Wiccans, witches, and other pagans often bring nature into their magickal workings. They time their rituals in accordance with nature's cycles and may include herbs, crystals, shells, and other natural ingredients in their spells. Their magick draws upon the forces of heaven and earth, as well as their own personal power, to create outcomes.

Ritual magicians (also called ceremonial or "high" magicians) engage in more intricate and formalized rituals, as their name implies. Many of their concepts are based on the teachings of the mystery schools in ancient Egypt and the Middle East. The Hebrew Kabbalah and the doctrines of Hermes Trismegistus play an important role in this type of magick, along with astrology, alchemy, and the tarot.

Shamans are adept at moving between the various worlds of existence, and can interact with beings who reside in the nonphysical realms. They journey to other worlds—in dreams or trance states, sometimes with the aid of spirit animals and guardians—to gain wisdom for healing, guidance, or protection.

These are just a few of the many magickal traditions that exist throughout the world. You may want to study more about magick's many faces and forms to determine which suits you best. Each has its own unique style, but you don't have to stick to just one. Take what you like and leave the rest. Most of the spells in this book are of the Celtic Wiccan/pagan variety, with a little shamanism, feng shui, and other stuff blended in.

THE RIGHT WAY VS. THE WRONG WAY

As you may have guessed, not all magick is good, and there are right and wrong ways to do it. In either case, unless you follow some fundamental procedures, you won't get the result you desire. Moreover, if you don't implement a few safety measures, you could endanger yourself or others.

Different schools of magick use different tools and techniques to generate outcomes. They may also subscribe to different codes of ethics. Generally speaking, however, most witches observe one basic rule: do no harm. Most also agree with the old saying "what goes around comes around."

Magick is not a game. Even the "k" is added to distinguish the real thing from card tricks and stage illusion. It can certainly be fun—just remember to respect its power.

WHITE, BLACK, AND GRAY MAGICK

You may have heard of white witches, meaning they uphold the "do no harm" rule. But the truth is, most magick isn't black or white, it's gray—including the magick most self-proclaimed white witches perform. That doesn't mean it's bad. In fact, all the spells in this book fall into the gray area. Just so we understand each other, let's define these three grades of magick:

- ✦ **BLACK MAGICK:** anything done to harm or manipulate another person or to interfere with his or her free will is black magick.
- ✳ **WHITE MAGICK:** white magick's purpose is to further spiritual growth, by strengthening your connection with the Divine realm and/or gaining wisdom from a higher source.
- ✶ **GRAY MAGICK:** everything else.

This means if you do a spell to get a better job or to attract a date, you're operating in the gray zone. Nothing wrong with that! But watch out, because it's easy to inadvertently cast a questionable spell—especially when you're having a bad day. Let's say your roommate is driving you crazy and you do a spell to get even with her for a dirty deed. Your revenge may seem justifiable, but it's still black magick.

Here's another little-known fact: most black magick isn't performed by evil sorcerers or wicked wizards—it's done by ordinary people who don't even realize what they're up to. Have you ever cursed some jerk for stealing your parking space or cutting ahead of you in a long line? That's black magick too.

One more fact: magick is all in your mind. As we discussed earlier in this chapter, magick involves forming an intention in your mind, then fueling it with energy and emotion. So if you wish for something hurtful to happen and invest that wish with angry emotions, you're doing black magick whether or not you enact a formal spellcasting ritual.

Maybe you're wondering why *not* to use magick to put someone who's wronged you in his place. It's tempting, for sure. Except that in the world of magick, whatever you do returns to you like a boomerang. That's a good reason for keeping your thoughts focused on positive stuff. It's also why usually the best way to get what you want—especially on days when everything seems to be going wrong—is to bless instead of curse.

FIGURE OUT WHAT YOU ACTUALLY WANT

Admittedly, it can be hard sometimes to determine if you're treading on the dark side of Magick Street. For many people, love spells seem to raise the most questions. What if you want to do a spell to get your yoga instructor to fall for you? Is that okay? It all depends on your intention. If he already has a partner and your goal is to steal him away, obviously that's not a good idea. But if he's single it's okay to use magick to get him to notice you, and later in this book you'll find a spell for that very purpose.

Good spells respect other people's free will and right to make their own choices in life. Even if your yoga teacher isn't romantically involved with anybody else, it's manipulative to cast a spell to coerce him into doing something he wouldn't want to do otherwise. How would you feel if someone did that to you?

There's another reason, too, to think carefully before casting a spell to win a person's heart. A well-executed spell creates a strong bond between you. Later on, if you change your mind, breaking the bond could be tough, to say the least.

Instead, look for another angle to accomplish your goal. You could magickally enhance your own attractiveness. You could do magick to remove any obstacles existing between you and the other person. You could do a spell to attract a partner who's right for you, rather than targeting a particular individual. Or you could turn the final decision over to a higher power by ending your spell with the words: "This is done in harmony with Divine Will, our own true wills, and for the benefit of all concerned." Witches often complete spells with a qualifying phrase like this to ensure their actions will produce positive results. No one can foresee all the surrounding circumstances, future possibilities, and karmic conditions involved in a situation. Maybe you and your yoga teacher would live happily ever after together. But maybe you'd be better off with somebody else—maybe someone you haven't even met yet. If your intention is that your spell will manifest "for the good of all, harming none," you're in the clear.

WHAT YOU SEE IS WHAT YOU'LL GET

When doing magick, it's important to know what you actually want and what achieving your goals looks like to you. Before you can attract money, a job, or a significant other, you must create a mental image of what you intend to manifest. If you're unsure of your goal before you start, what you get may not be what you want.

Magick spells utilize both the conscious and the subconscious parts of your mind, aligning them so they work together in tandem. Whether you realize it or not, your subconscious is always busy influencing your everyday activities, decisions, and interactions with other people—sometimes in ways that conflict with your conscious plans. If the conscious and subconscious aren't on the same page, the result will not be what you were hoping for.

In magick, a picture really is worth a thousand words. Witches often use a technique called "creative visualization" by which the conscious mind formulates a precise mental picture of the end result you wish to manifest. This picture shows the subconscious what you want it to help bring about. In the next chapter, you'll learn to design effective visualizations. You'll also explore ways to incorporate imagery into your spells—because what you see is what you'll get.

A WORD OF CAUTION

Abracadabra. The word is synonymous with magick. It comes from the Aramaic *Avarah K'Davarah* meaning "I will create as I speak." When you speak, your words vibrate through the space around you and subtly affect everything they touch.

Like images, words influence the subconscious and direct it to fulfill your intentions. In order to get the results you desire, however, you have to ask in the right way. When you're formulating magick spells, you must state exactly what you wish to achieve, in precise, uncomplicated terms. Otherwise the outcome might not be what you'd hoped for. Your subconscious hears everything you say, and interprets your words in a rather simplistic, linear way. So if you say, "I'm too fat," or, "I couldn't do that in a million years," your subconscious will strive to make your words come true. Conversely, you can use positive statements to magickally create positive results.

Start paying attention to what you say and how you say it. In the next chapter, you'll learn several techniques for incorporating words into magick spells and rituals. Later in this book you'll find lots of spells that utilize words to shape and empower your intentions.

MAKE A MAGICK CIRCLE

If you wanted to keep your dog in your yard and keep other dogs out, you'd put up a fence. When you're doing spells, you contain magickal energy and prevent outside interferences from getting in by erecting a magick "fence" known as a circle. Circle-casting techniques range from very simple to elegant. The quick and easy method is to just envision a circle of white light surrounding you and the area where you'll perform your spell. Some people like to draw a circle on the ground with flour, chalk, or another temporary medium. Others arrange candles or crystals in a circle around the perimeter of the magick space. It's really up to you which method you decide to use, and you don't always have to use the same one. However, casting a circle the right way involves a few basic steps.

1. Clear the space of any unwanted energies. The simplest way to do this is with a broom—sweep the air as well as the floor. As you sweep, say aloud: "This space is now cleared of all harmful, disruptive, and unwanted energies."
2. Light a stick of sage or a bundled sage wand and allow the fragrant smoke to waft through the area to purify it.
3. Bring everything you'll need for the spell into the area around which you'll cast the circle.
4. Position yourself so that when you've completed the circle you'll be inside it.
5. Start at the east and move in a clockwise direction until you've completed the circle and returned to the east. If you're lighting candles, for instance, light the easternmost candle first and continue working clockwise until they're all burning. If you're using a magick wand to draw the circle, begin by aiming the wand toward the east and turn in a clockwise direction, holding the wand straight out horizontal to the earth, until you've gone 360 degrees around.
6. Once the circle has been cast, don't leave it until you've finished your spell.
7. When you're finished doing the spell, open the circle. Go back to the east and move in a counterclockwise direction, reversing your earlier steps. Extinguish the candles one by one, erase the chalk line, douse the burning sage, and

so forth. This allows your magick to flow out into the universe and take effect.

WHO'S IN YOUR MAGICKAL SQUAD?

Most witches believe we aren't alone in this universe—we share it with myriad nonphysical beings, including lots of good guys who are willing to help us. They guide, protect, and aid us in our daily lives. When things go wrong, we can call on them for assistance.

Some people envision these divine helpers as angels. Others prefer to think of them as sages, guardians, or parts of their own higher consciousness. Native Americans often look to revered ancestors and spirit animals for guidance. Pagans frequently request help from various gods and goddesses. Faeries and nature spirits, elementals, and extraterrestrials might also bring you benefits. However you choose to view these entities, they can be tremendous assets in magickal work—indeed, they could be essential to a spell's success.

When working with spirit helpers, certain rules of etiquette apply:

✷ **SHOW RESPECT**—treat spirit helpers as honored teachers and allies, not servants.

✦ **ASK FOR ASSISTANCE**—guides, guardians, and deities recognize your free will and might not intervene unless you invite them to do so.

✷ **DON'T TRY TO MICROMANAGE**—if you seek aid from spirit beings, turn over the reins and allow them to carry out your request as they see fit.

✦ **DON'T SEEK HELP TO DO HARM**—although there are some evil entities out there, you don't want to join forces with them, and the good spirits won't get behind a bad cause.

✳ **EXPRESS GRATITUDE**—remember to thank the beings who assist you, and perhaps give them an offering.

KEEP GOOD RECORDS

Witches often write down their spells in what's called a *grimoire*, or book of shadows. This record describes in detail what ingredients were used, what actions or procedures were implemented, for whom the spells were performed, and what results occurred. Remember to date each entry too.

It's not usually a good idea to show anyone else what you've written in your book of spells. Stash your grimoire in a safe place or write in code to keep your secrets safe.

Keeping track of your spells allows you to see what turned out well and, if necessary, what you want to tweak a bit. You'll probably decide to repeat a successful spell again and again, like a favorite recipe, so don't risk forgetting what went into it.

PRACTICE MAKES PERFECT

Like anything, magick requires practice to perfect. Training your mind takes time—it can be harder to build mental muscles than physical ones. Don't give up if your efforts don't produce immediate results. Keep trying and see mistakes as learning opportunities.

Here are a few tips that can help you develop your magickal skills and power:

- ✦ **USE YOUR SENSES**—burn incense, listen to soothing music, and so on.
- ✳ **PAY ATTENTION TO YOUR INTUITION**—hunches, epiphanies, vivid dreams, serendipitous experiences, and so on will increase in frequency as you start opening up to them.
- ✳ **KEEP YOUR GRIMOIRE UP-TO-DATE**—keeping track of your successes and failures will help you remember what to do—or what not to do—next time you try a spell.
- ✳ **ELIMINATE AS MANY DISTRACTIONS AS POSSIBLE**—turn off the TV, radio, computer, and phone when doing magick. Try to work when you know you won't get interrupted or sidetracked.
- ✦ **EXPERIMENT WITH DIFFERENT TYPES OF MAGICK**—some may appeal to you more than others. Gardeners usually enjoy herbal magick; artists excel at visual spells.
- ✳ **WORK WHEN YOUR ENERGY IS HIGH**—some of us are morning people, others are night owls. Do magick when you feel strong and alert, not when you're stressed out, tired, sad, or ill.
- ✦ **READ OTHER BOOKS**—and if possible, talk to other practitioners. Exposing yourself to a variety of ideas will help you determine what's best for you.

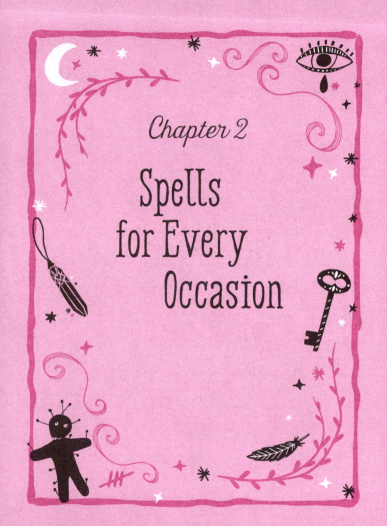

Chapter 2

Spells for Every Occasion

In the world of magick, all the power is in your hands! There's always more than one way to do your thing, so you can easily choose what works best for you. No matter the occasion, you can be sure there's a spell for it. And if you're having trouble finding one that's exactly right, you can customize any spell to fit a specific situation. You can even combine two, three, or more spells to get exactly what you need. Infuse a magick potion with visual imagery. Add a written affirmation to a talisman. Magick isn't really about the format of the spell; it's all about the energy you put into it. The trick is to engage your mind, emotions, and senses as much as possible. This chapter will teach you everything you need to know about different kinds of spells and when and how to use them.

VISUAL SPELLS

All spells originate in the mind's eye. If you're naturally a visual person with a terrific imagination, you're already a step ahead. Artists, writers, and other creative individuals often excel at magick—in fact, some of the world's most noted artists, like William Blake and William Butler Yeats, were practitioners.

You needn't be a master artist to be a master spellcaster. The truth is, you're always creating images in your mind. Notice what happens when you read the word *camel*. You immediately pictured a large, long-legged animal with a hump, right?

Creative visualization isn't just daydreaming, and it's more than pretty pictures. You'll need to follow a few simple rules to get it to work for you. Here are some tips for creating successful and powerful visualizations:

* Choose an image or scenario that depicts your objective clearly, without ambiguity.
* Make sure to put yourself in the picture; otherwise, the end result might transpire without you.
* Include only positive imagery in your visualization.
* Add action, color, sounds, smells, and other sensory cues to enhance the scene and make your image more vibrant.
* Don't try to figure out all the steps leading up to the outcome, just visualize the end result.

Let's say you want to take a dream vacation in Rome. You could create a picture of yourself standing at the Colosseum on a beautiful sunny day, or eating pasta with a delightful companion at a trattoria near the Spanish Steps. Give your imagination free rein—really *feel* yourself enjoying every aspect of the experience. Hold the image in your mind while you cast your spell.

If your objective is to transform a bad situation into a good one, form an image of what you want to happen—don't think about the problems you're trying to overcome. For example, if you're doing a spell to mend a broken arm, don't envision the injury. Instead, see the arm whole, healthy, and functioning perfectly.

A Little Help for Visual Spells

You don't have to rely totally on your own imagination to conjure up images. It's okay to use ready-made pictures or to reinforce your own visualizations with material from other sources. For instance, cut out magazine photos that depict your desires and post them where you'll see them often. Looking at these images regularly trains your subconscious to produce what it sees. Is your old computer ready for the museum? Place a photo of a new model you'd like to own on your desk to help you attract the real thing.

You can download visuals from the Internet, too, and use them as screensavers. Or, combine a series of images to make a magickal slide show. Assemble your own digital photo album of pictures you want to view regularly.

How Do Visual Spells Work?

Visuals can enhance any spell, so long as they accurately depict your intentions. Here are some ways to tap the power of images in your spells:

★ Slip an image that illustrates your desire into a mojo bag.

✳ Draw a design on a candle—as the candle burns, it releases your intention into the universe.

➤ Set a quartz crystal on top of a picture—the crystal will transmit the energy of the image where you want it to go.

✳ Put a glass of water on top of a picture—the water will absorb the image. Drink the imprinted water.

Many of the spells in this book include visuals, but don't limit yourself to the suggestions offered here. Use your imagination to devise other methods that suit your purposes.

VERBAL SPELLS

Verbal spells are among the simplest and quickest types of magick. Quite likely, the earliest spells were spoken charms requesting favors from deities. Some spells contain strange-sounding words, such as angelic names from ancient languages. Many magick rituals include statements, rhymes, chants, songs, or prayers.

Words help focus your mind and clarify your intention. Spoken words also produce sounds that resonate through your body and your environment—the sound waves influence the energy patterns to generate effects. Written words bring your intention out of the realm of thought and make it physical.

Affirmations

Affirmations are short, positive statements designed to generate an outcome. You can write affirmations or say them aloud. Repeating an affirmation regularly reprograms your mind and replaces old beliefs with new ones. Used in spell-working, affirmations tell your subconscious what you want it to do. As you probably guessed, there's an art to writing successful affirmations. These tips will help you get it right:

✳ Word the affirmation in the present tense, as if the outcome you desire already exists.

✦ Keep it short and simple.

➤ Be precise—ambiguous or unclear statements may produce mixed results.

➤ Keep the focus on you, making sure to include yourself in your statement.

✳ State the affirmation in positive terms, using words that convey desired conditions.

✦ Describe only the outcome you want to achieve—don't worry about the steps necessary to get there.

For example, a protection affirmation should be worded "I am safe and sound at all times and in all situations," not "Nobody will harm me." See the difference?

Incantations

An affirmation that rhymes is called an incantation. Witches often prefer incantations because the rhyme and rhythm make them easy to remember. The same guidelines apply in both cases. Short and sweet is usually best; however, incantations may be longer than non-rhyming affirmations. If you like, you can even set an incantation to music. Don't worry too much about your poetry-writing skills. A simple, catchy, clearly worded rhyme will be more effective than an elegant ode.

Let's try rewriting a protection affirmation as an incantation. Here's one possibility:

"In all I do throughout the day
I am safe in every way."

Words Have Power

The creation stories of many cultures describe words as being the instruments of manifestation. Although all words have creative potential, some are believed to contain special power. Meditators, for example, intone the word *Om* because its healing frequencies balance mind and body.

One of the shortest statements is also one of the most powerful: "I am." When you utter these words, you draw upon your own higher power for creative purposes. Speak this phrase with great care and pay attention to whatever words follow—*never* say things like "I am fat/stupid/ugly/sick and tired/bad at handling money," and so on. Your affirmation is likely to materialize.

When casting a spell, it's customary to repeat an intention three times. Three is a magick number that brings the spell into the three-dimensional world. You may also choose to add a final command at the end of a spell, such as "So be it now" or "So mote it be," to show you mean business!

Using Words in Spellwork

Of course, speaking an affirmation, incantation, or prayer is the most common form of verbal spellworking. However, you can tap the power of words in lots of other ways too:

- Write your intention on a piece of paper, then burn the paper to release and activate your wish.
- Write an affirmation or incantation on a slip of paper and insert it into a talisman or amulet.
- Inscribe a word that encapsulates your objective on a candle—as the candle burns, it releases your intention into the universe.
- Write words such as *love*, *peace*, and *joy* on a piece of paper, then tape the paper to a bottle of water. The word charges the water with its energy, creating a magick potion.

BURNING SPELLS

You may not realize it, but you've probably already done burning spells. Lighting candles on a birthday cake and making a wish is a simple magick spell. So is lighting a novena candle to ask a deity for favors. Fire, in one form or another, plays a role in many of our familiar celebrations and rituals, both secular and spiritual. That's because fire represents the divine spark that enlivens matter, the spirit that abides in each of us.

Burning spells serve two purposes, which may seem contradictory. They create and they destroy; they attract and they banish. You can burn a written request or symbol to attract something you desire, or to eliminate something you don't want from your life. The act of burning releases your intention into the universe, so it can be acted upon.

Candle Magick

Candle spells are among the most popular and beloved forms of magick. Because candles are so versatile, they're included in many of the spells in this book. Here are some ways you can use candles to work magick:

* Choose a candle of a color that represents your goal, then burn it to activate your wish.
* Let a candle symbolize a person, object, or intention.
* Arrange candles in a circle to provide protection while you're doing magick.

Pillar candles are ideal for rituals, because they burn for hours. They're good for spells that require repetition over a period of days. Tapers provide ambiance and dress up your magick space. Use novena or tealight candles for short spells.

It's a good idea to wash your candles before using them to remove any unwanted energies they may have picked up along the way. "Dressing" a candle with essential oils is also a common practice, performed to dedicate the candle to your goal and trigger your subconscious.

Incense

In many religious ceremonies, incense is burned to perfume the air and to send prayers to the heavens. Incense is also burned as an offering to deities. Witches burn certain scents for certain purposes—rose or jasmine for love spells, mint for money spells, cinnamon or sandalwood for success, and so on. Here are some other ways to use incense:

* Light sage incense to clear a space of unwanted energies before performing a spell or ritual.
* Cast a circle by trailing incense smoke around the circumference of a space you want to sanctify and protect.
* Charge talismans, amulets, and magick tools by holding them in incense smoke.

Balefire

Traditionally, balefires were built in circular, outdoor pits during ceremonies and rites. Today, a barbecue grill, hibachi, or fireplace could be an adequate substitute. Fire spells are still performed by witches to spark creativity, abundance, and purification in many forms. Here are some other suggestions for effective fire spells:

* Write a wish on a piece of paper and drop it in a balefire to activate your intention.
* Burn a symbol of something you want to eliminate (such as a bad habit or illness) in a balefire.
* Fabricate an effigy of someone you want to be free of and burn it to dissolve the attachment.

MAGICK MOJOS

When African slaves were transported to the United States they brought their magickal traditions with them. Among those was the *mojo*, which derives from the Congolese word *moyo* meaning "soul" or "life force." Although any charm can loosely be called a mojo, the term usually refers to a cloth bag filled with herbs, stones, prayers, and other lucky ingredients.

You can fashion a mojo either to draw something you desire to you or to ward off something you don't want around. These two types of charms go by different names. *Talismans* attract blessings and benefits. *Amulets* repel unpleasant circumstances, people, or energies. Later in this book you'll learn how to make both. Here are just a few ways to use mojos:

* Carry an amulet in your pocket for protection.
* Place a love talisman under your pillow to attract a partner.
* Put a money mojo in your cash register or safe to increase prosperity.

According to some belief systems, you must feed a mojo if you want it to continue working its magick. Dab a drop of essential oil on it periodically to keep its power going strong.

POTIONS AND LOTIONS

Potions and lotions—tonics, oils, ointments, teas, and so on—are used widely for healing purposes. Some potions and lotions contain ingredients with obvious curative properties, such as a cold salve with camphor added. Others work through resonance and include no measurable plant substance. The good news is that most magick potions contain ordinary ingredients you can find in any supermarket.

In the following chapters, you'll learn how to make magick potions and lotions for a variety of reasons. Some incorporate herbs, plant oils, or fruit juice; others rely only on your thoughts for their power. Here are some ways to enjoy magick potions and lotions:

- Share a love potion served in a ritual chalice with your partner.
- Dab a drop of magick lotion on an amulet or talisman to charge it.
- Sip a health potion throughout the day to enhance well-being.
- Mist the air with a scented potion to promote peace and relaxation.

Use caution when working with magick potions and lotions. Even natural ingredients can produce allergic reactions and some botanicals are toxic if ingested. Test essential oils before applying them to skin, as some can cause irritation.

SYMPATHETIC MAGICK

Sympathetic magick relies on what's known as the "law of similars" by employing methods or materials that resemble the outcome you desire. For example, a spell to attract money might call for planting coins in the ground to make your bank account grow. Here are some other examples of sympathetic magick:

- To boost courage, design a ritual in which you wear a lion mask and roar like a lion.
- To sever an unwanted bond, tie two cords together, then cut the cords with scissors.
- Stand under a shower to cleanse yourself of an unwanted condition, habit, or emotion.

One popular form of sympathetic magick involves the use of dolls or poppets. These figurines are created to represent people or occasionally nonphysical entities. Whatever you do to the doll symbolizes what you intend to do to the person it represents. If you wanted to heal a broken leg, you'd place a splint on the poppet's leg. You can fashion a poppet of cloth, wax, wood, clay, straw, or other material. Dress and decorate it to resemble the person it represents. (Forget about those stereotypical voodoo dolls, however—poking pins in a poppet to cause someone pain is black magick.)

RITUALS AND RITES

Our lives are full of rituals—getting ready in the morning, driving to work, preparing meals, working out at the gym, heading to bed at night—that lend order to our days. Holiday rituals connect us with our heritage and the wheel of the year. Religious rituals transport us from the mundane into the spiritual realm.

A ritual is a formula, a series of prescribed steps leading to a desired outcome. Magick rituals focus your mind and build energy that can be directed toward your goal. Words, movements, ambiance, clothing, objects, etc., all contribute to the ritual's purpose.

Spells are rituals. So are rites and celebrations. All rites are rituals but not all rituals are rites. As a general distinction, rites usually mark an event, time, or passage of significance and frequently include a spiritual and/or ceremonial aspect.

You already have experience creating rituals and rites. You've probably planned birthday, graduation, or anniversary celebrations, holiday festivities, maybe even a wedding. Designing a magick ritual or rite follows pretty much the same steps, and you can design a ritual or rite for just about anything. Use your imagination. The more thought and enthusiasm you put into your ritual, the more meaning it will have for you and the other participants—and the more powerful it will be.

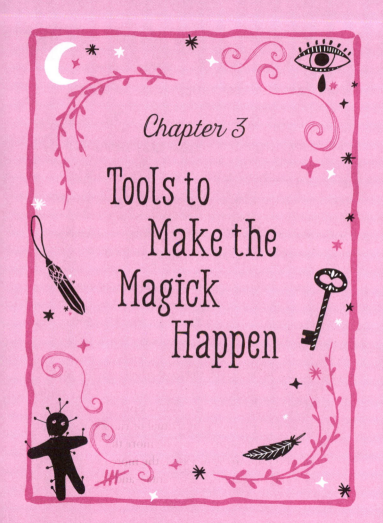

Chapter 3

Tools to Make the Magick Happen

It should be no surprise that witches use special tools in their spellwork. Magick wands, anyone? But you may be less familiar with the other tools witches often use. Often, the tool's symbolism is what's really important for deciding when and how it will be most effective. The four primary magick tools (the wand, pentagram, athame, and chalice) symbolize the four elements (fire, earth, air, and water, respectively). If you want to stabilize your finances, you might use the pentagram (symbol of earth) in your spellworking. If you want to fan the flames in a romantic relationship, the wand (symbol of fire) could have a role in your ritual. Of course, you don't really need tools to perform magick—it's all about willpower and energy—but they can be a useful way to strengthen your skills, improve your focus, and help your spells be even more successful.

THE MAGICK WAND

A wand's main purpose is to direct energy. If you want to send energy to a person, place, or thing, just aim your magick wand in that direction and presto—there it goes! You can also attract energy with a wand—point it at the sky to draw down power from the heavens, or at the ground to draw up the energy of Mother Earth. Witches often cast protective circles (see Chapter 1) around a designated space by using a wand to direct energy.

According to tradition, a wand should be at least 6 inches long, but only as big as is comfortable to handle. Early wands were wooden, cut from the branch of a tree the witch considered sacred (yew, rowan, and willow were favorites). Today, however, you can find wands made of metal, glass, and other materials. The wand corresponds to the element of fire.

THE PENTAGRAM

A pentagram is a five-pointed star with a circle around it. The correct way to display it is with one point upright, two points down, and two out to the sides to represent the human body. Witches use the pentagram for protection. You can inscribe pentagrams on candles, paint them on stones, embroider them on mojo pouches and clothing—just about any place. The pentagram corresponds to the element of earth.

THE ATHAME

This ritual dagger is never used for practical purposes (such as chopping vegetables) and certainly not to harm someone.

Rather, a witch symbolically slices away negative energy or cuts through obstacles with this magick tool.

An athame is usually a double-sided knife about 4–6 inches long. It doesn't have to be sharp, however, because you won't cut anything physical with it. Remember, that your athame is a weapon of the "spiritual warrior" and tradition says you shouldn't work with a knife that has drawn blood. The athame corresponds to the element of air.

THE CHALICE

The most famous chalice of all is the legendary Holy Grail. As you might suspect, a chalice is used for drinking beverages—but not your everyday kind. Your chalice should only hold ritual brews and magick potions. In some rituals, a ceremonial drink is passed among participants, which is why chalices often have long stems that are easy to grasp. A chalice may be made of any material: silver, gold, copper, crystal, glass, ceramic, even wood. The chalice corresponds to the element of water.

OTHER MAGICK TOOLS (OPTIONAL)

You might eventually decide to add more magickal implements to your collection. Some of the spells in the following chapters utilize various tools for special purposes. Brooms are used to sweep unwanted energies from a ritual space. Bells, gongs, drums, and rattles raise positive energy and disperse bad vibes. Swords banish harmful forces and slice through obstacles. Staffs (or staves) direct energy.

Although it's often connected with witches, the cauldron is a handy tool for any practitioner. If you don't have a fireplace, balefire pit, or barbecue grill, you can build a small ritual fire in a cauldron. You can also concoct magick brews or cook ceremonial meals in it. The traditional cauldron is made of iron, but yours might be fashioned from ceramic, copper, stainless steel, stone, or another fireproof material.

Many witches use divination devices to see beyond the manifest world. Pendulums and crystal balls provide glimpses into the unknown. Tarot cards are popular tools for reading the future. Runes, too, can guide your path; they also play roles in spells.

CLEANING AND CHARGING YOUR MAGICK TOOLS

Before you use a tool for magickal purposes, it's a good idea to clean it. Cleaning removes unwanted energies, as well as dust and dirt. In most cases the easiest way to do this is to wash the item with mild soap and water. If you prefer, you can "smudge" your tools by holding them in the smoke from burning sage or incense for a few moments.

The next step is called "charging." A magick ritual in itself, charging consecrates your tools for magickal purposes and imprints them with your intentions. One popular method for doing this involves the four elements: earth, air, fire, and water. Mix a little sea salt in water and sprinkle it on the tool as you say to it: "With earth and water I charge you to do my will." Then, light incense and hold the tool in the smoke for a few moments while you say: "With fire and air I charge you to do my will." (Make sure to dry metal tools after sprinkling them with salt water so they don't tarnish or corrode.)

Another technique calls for anointing your tools with essential oils. Rub a little essential oil on the implement while you say: "With this oil I charge you to do my will."

MAGICK TOOL	ESSENTIAL OILS FOR CHARGING
Wand	cinnamon, sandalwood, clove, musk, patchouli, cedar
Pentagram	mint, pine, amber, basil, fennel, anise
Athame	carnation, lavender, ginger, honeysuckle
Chalice	rose, ylang-ylang, jasmine

These suggestions are just that: suggestions. Feel free to design a more elaborate or personal ritual for charging your magick tools. The purpose is to make these tools yours, so the more personal the ritual the better.

CARING FOR YOUR MAGICK TOOLS

Many magicians prefer to store their tools safely out of sight, partly to prevent other people from handling them and partly to avoid uncomfortable questions. It's traditional to wrap your magick tools in silk. You might choose instead to put them in velvet pouches, wooden boxes, or other containers and stash them in a drawer, trunk, or cabinet. When caring for your tools, here are a few precautions and protocols to remember:

- ✦ Don't let anyone else use your tools or handle them, except perhaps a magickal partner with whom you work regularly.
- ✳ If someone else does touch a tool, smudge or wash it to remove that person's energy.
- ✦ Clean and smudge all tools before you begin using them to perform magick. After that, you needn't cleanse them unless someone else touches them. (Of course, if you drink or eat from a chalice or cauldron you'll want to wash it before storing it.)

SETTING UP AN ALTAR

If you plan on doing magick frequently—and why wouldn't you?—you might like to erect a permanent altar in your home. An altar can be a simple table draped with a beautiful cloth, an ornate antique cabinet with lots of drawers, or anything in between. Many people use their altars to hold their magickal implements. You might also like to display candles, crystals, statues of favorite deities, flowers, and other meaningful objects there. Some of the spells in the following chapters recommend leaving spell components on your altar for a period of time.

However, an altar is more than a piece of furniture for storing your treasures. It establishes a sanctuary in your home. You go there to temporarily leave the ordinary, everyday world behind and enter a magickal space.

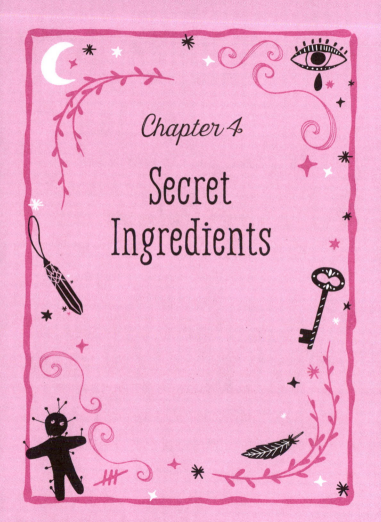

Chapter 4

Secret Ingredients

Here's good news for the first-time spellcaster: there's no need to hunt out crazy ingredients to make spells work. Today's spells usually consist of ordinary ingredients that you can find in any supermarket, health food store, or department store. What makes these everyday items magickal? It's actually something called *resonance* combined with the intention you set. *Resonance* is the vibrational quality of something that distinguishes it. In spellworking, you choose items whose resonance gives them a synchronous relationship with your intention. It's a little tricky, but without even knowing it, you're already familiar with synchronous relationships. Roses, for instance, are connected with love. As you become more adept at magick, you'll intuitively sense what to use in a spell to produce the desired result. Until that time, refer to the charts and tables in this chapter.

NOTE

While you'll see exact measurements for some ingredients throughout the spells, you'll notice that a lot of the measurements have been left up to you. You're the one creating and casting the spell so use your intuition and power when adding the items; you'll know when enough is enough.

CHOOSE THE RIGHT COLOR

Even if you aren't aware of it, the colors in your environment affect you psychologically and physically. Studies show that people respond to colors in measurable ways. For example, test subjects placed in red rooms often feel warmer and more active than those placed in blue rooms.

We also attach symbolic meanings to colors. Green reminds us of grass, leaves, crops in the fields, and by association, growth. We even use colors to describe moods with expressions like "feeling blue." These subconscious connections with color can be tapped in spellworking.

The easiest way to bring color into a spell is with candles. Candle magick is a popular type of spellcasting, and you can incorporate candles into virtually any spell or ritual.

You can also burn candles of different colors to fine-tune a spell. Let's say you hate your job and want to find a better one. If money is an object (and it usually is), you'll need a green or gold candle. If you're also looking for a position of leadership or power, add a purple candle. And if you'd like fun and excitement in the package, use an orange candle.

COLOR	CORRESPONDENCES
Red	passion, vitality, courage, action
Orange	confidence, success
Yellow	happiness, creativity
Green	fertility, growth, wealth, health
Light blue	peace, clarity, soothing
Royal blue	independence, insight, imagination
Indigo	intuition, serenity, mental power
Purple	power, authority, wisdom
Pink	love, friendship
White	purity, protection
Black	power, wisdom, banishing
Brown	stability, practicality

When you're making magick mojos, choose bags in colors that are appropriate to your intention. To give detail to your spell, tie the bag with a ribbon of a different color. Pink is the obvious choice for a love talisman. But if you'd like passion in the mix, use a red ribbon. Ritual clothing, altar cloths, flowers, and other accessories can also provide color during spellworking. Use your imagination to heighten the sensory aspects of a spell.

USE SOME FLOWER POWER

"Green magick" has long been a favorite form of spellcraft. Early herbalists knew the secrets of the plant kingdom and how to use botanicals to cure and conjure. Because plants are living entities, they bring their own energies to a spell. In some cases, you might choose a particular herb or flower for its physical properties—especially if you're doing healing. More often, however, you're looking for the symbolic value of the botanicals you use in spells. Roses, of course, are symbols of love. Pine, which stays green even in winter, represents endurance and longevity.

Just about any part of the plant—flowers, leaves, bark, seeds, and roots—can be used in your spells. If you have a green thumb, you can grow your own plants for magick work. But if not you can find most of what you'll need at a nursery or large supermarket.

You can capture the power of flowers and other botanicals in incense, essential oils, teas, lotions, or by keeping live plants in your home. Here are some ways you might like to use plants in spells:

* Burn herbs, bark, or sticks of wood in a ritual fire.
* Wear essential oils that suit your purposes.
* Blend healing plant oils into lotions, salves, and ointments.

Use caution when handling plant material. Some favorite magickal flowers, such as foxglove and wolfsbane, are poisonous. Don't put anything you aren't sure of in food or beverages—stick with common kitchen herbs. Even plants that seem benign may cause allergic reactions in some people.

PLANT	USES
Ash	For protection and banishing
Basil	For protection
Bay laurel	For love, success and victory, and to protect your home
Cayenne	To stimulate courage or sexual desire
Cedar	For wealth and success
Chamomile	For peace of mind or to calm a stressful situation; drink chamomile tea as a relaxing digestive or sleep aid
Cinnamon	For financial and career success, in love spells
Clove	For success and prosperity, to remove negativity
Comfrey	For protection and purification
Daisy	For good luck and happiness
Fennel	For protection
Frankincense	For meditation, to heighten intuition
Garlic	For protection; eat to cleanse the system
Ginger	To make a spell work faster, especially a love spell
Jasmine	To attract love and passion, to sweeten an unpleasant situation
Lavender	To promote relaxation, to ease stress

PLANT	USES
Marigold	For success in legal or financial matters
Marjoram	To ease stress during big changes
Mint	For prosperity
Nettle	To dispel malice, gossip, and envy
Parsley	For prosperity
Pine	For strength and longevity
Rose	For love
Rosemary	For protection
Sage	To clear the air and remove negative energy
Tarragon	To inspire compassion and congeniality
Thyme	For fun and happiness

Remember, the more essential oil you add the stronger the scent will be, so if you would rather a lighter scent, go easy on the amount you add. Concentrated essential oils can bother sensitive skin, and you should always test lotions on a small area of skin before applying in case of irritation.

ADD SOME CRYSTALS AND GEMSTONES

From earliest times, people around the world have esteemed crystals and gemstones for their magickal properties. Like plants, crystals and gemstones are living entities, although they resonate at a rate that most people can't perceive.

However, their slow, concentrated energy enables them to keep working their magick for a long period of time. You can include crystals or gemstones in virtually any spell to increase, focus, stabilize, or fine-tune its power.

Quartz crystals are the most versatile. When combined with other stones or herbs they amplify the qualities of those ingredients. Witches sometimes use crystals as wands to direct energy. You could:

* Put them in amulets or talismans.
* Set them near windows and doors to provide protection.
* Infuse magick potions with them.

Different stones possess different qualities and serve different functions in spellworking. A stone's color can provide clues to its abilities. Pink gems, such as rose quartz and morganite, are perfect for love spells. Jade, aventurine, and other green stones can benefit money spells.

If you wish, combine several stones to address various aspects of a spell. If your goal is to find a job that pays well and brings you into contact with interesting people—aventurine plus watermelon tourmaline should do the trick.

Remember to wash crystals and gemstones in mild soap and water before using them to do magick. Stones hold on to vibrations for a long time and you don't want other people's energies to interfere with your spells.

STONE	USES
Amber	For protection
Amethyst	For meditation, relaxation, dream recall, and heightening intuition
Aquamarine	For mental clarity and spiritual insight
Aventurine	For prosperity
Bloodstone	For strength, courage, and physical protection
Citrine	To clean other stones and crystals, to disperse unwanted energies
Coral	To attract love or friendship
Diamond	For commitment in a relationship, for strength and success
Emerald	For love spells, healing, or growth in any area
Hematite	For stability or permanence
Jade	For prosperity or health
Jasper	Red jasper stimulates passion in love spells; green or rainforest jasper supports growth and healing
Lapis lazuli	To increase insight and intuition
Moldavite	For psychic ability or to communicate with other worlds
Moonstone	For emotional balance and intuition

STONE	USES
Morganite	To bring love into one's life and to rekindle old loves
Onyx	For banishing spells, for stability
Opal	To increase attractiveness in love spells, to protect a loved one
Pearl	For self-esteem, to help heal female or emotional problems
Quartz (clear)	To hold information, to boost the power of other stones, to transmit ideas and energy
Rose quartz	For love and friendship, to balance emotions
Ruby	To increase passion and vitality
Sapphire	To gain insight; star sapphires inspire hope
Smoky quartz	For endurance, focus, and practicality
Tiger's eye	For abundance of all kinds
Tourmaline	Green and black tourmaline remove negative energy; pink and watermelon tourmaline attract friends and helpful people
Turquoise	For protection and prosperity

SELECTING THE RIGHT ROPES AND RIBBONS

When you tie up a mojo bag, you're sealing the spell itself. In fact, tying knots is an ancient and effective form of magick. The idea is that you can capture energies, thoughts, and emotions in a knot. Sometimes you only want to contain energy for a period of time. When you need that energy, untie the knot and release it.

The number of knots you tie can be significant too. Love spells might call for two knots to represent the couple for whom the spell is cast. Four, the number of stability, could be appropriate in a money spell to slow the outflow of cash. Here are other ways to use ropes and ribbons in your spells:

✦ To hold the energy of blessings, prayers, or incantations.
✷ To connect two or more symbolic items.
✳ To bind an enemy.

Remember to consider a ribbon's color. As we discussed earlier, colors convey symbolic meanings.

SIGNS AND SYMBOLS

Magick relies heavily on the use of symbols. Symbols convey information to the subconscious quickly and efficiently. Numbers, icons, gestures, and geometric shapes are some of the symbols we utilize every day in our mundane lives. These symbols and others can also be used in spellworking. Witches often include runes or astrological glyphs in spells. Animal images, objects from nature, figurines, and even household items can serve symbolic purposes in spells. Consider incorporating symbols into your spells in these ways:

* Draw a symbol on a piece of paper and display it where you'll see it often.
* Include small symbolic objects in amulets and talismans.
* Carve symbols on candles.

You can even design your own original symbols. One way to do this is to draw what's known as a *sigil*. Choose a word that conveys your intention, such as *love*, *prosperity*, or *success*. Configure the letters in the word so they form a picture. Use upper or lower case letters, script or block, or a combination. Draw the letters right-side up or upside down, backwards or forwards, large or small—whatever strikes your fancy. When you're finished, you'll have an image that nobody but you will recognize. It's your own secret code! Both the act of creating the sigil and its application are magickal acts, so remember to approach the process in the right frame of mind.

OTHER INGREDIENTS

As you become more proficient at doing magick, you'll develop a sense of what things will enhance your spells. You might consider adding the element of sound with bells, drums, singing bowls, gongs, or chimes. The choice is entirely up to you. If an object inspires you or helps you get into the spirit of things, by all means, use it.

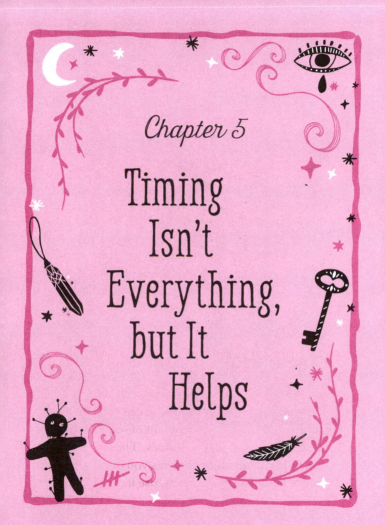

Chapter 5

Timing Isn't Everything, but It Helps

You've gathered your tools, selected the perfect ingredients, and know exactly what you want to accomplish with your spell. But how do you know *when* to start? If you're preparing for a new project or applying for a job, timing can be crucial to your success. The same is true with magick. By performing a spell or ritual on an auspicious date, you increase the likelihood of accomplishing your goal quickly and effectively. From the days of the week to some basic astrology to magickal holidays, there's a time and a place for everything, including magick!

EVERY DAY OF THE WEEK

Before powerful telescopes allowed astronomers to see beyond the range of the human eye, only seven heavenly bodies could be observed from Earth: the sun, the moon, Mercury, Venus, Mars, Jupiter, and Saturn. Early people believed that gods and goddesses inhabited these planets, which bear the names of their resident deities.

Each god or goddess was said to possess particular characteristics and preside over certain aspects of earthly life. According to ancient tradition, each deity's power reigned supreme on one of the seven days of the week. By scheduling activities on a day when the deity who ruled your particular interest was in charge, you could enhance your chances of success. When doing magick spells, the same holds true today, as seen in the following table. Love spells, for example, can benefit from the energy of Venus if you perform them on Friday.

MAGICK IN THE MOON

Witches know that you're more likely to reap the rewards you desire if you do spells during auspicious phases of the moon. When casting spells, pay particular attention to four significant lunar periods: the new moon, full moon, and waxing and waning phases.

The new moon, as you might expect, favors beginnings. Are you looking for a new job? A new romance? The best time to do spells to initiate a project, to start a journey, or to plant seeds—literally or figuratively—is during the new moon. As the moon grows in size, your project will grow too.

DAYS OF THE WEEK	RULING PLANET/DEITY	AREAS OF INFLUENCE
Monday	Moon	Fertility, creativity, home and family matters, intuition
Tuesday	Mars	Contests/competition, courage, strength/vitality, men
Wednesday	Mercury	Communication, commerce, intellectual concerns
Thursday	Jupiter	Growth/expansion, prosperity, travel
Friday	Venus	Love, partnerships, the arts, women
Saturday	Saturn	Limitations, authority, endurance, stability, protection
Sunday	Sun	Public image, confidence, career pursuits, well-being

The waxing moon—the two weeks after the new moon and leading up to the full moon—supports growth and expansion. Do you want to boost your income? Get a promotion at work? Cast your spell while the moon's light is increasing to generate growth in your worldly affairs.

The full moon marks a time of culmination. Want to bring a project to a successful conclusion? Receive rewards, recognition, or payments that are due to you? Do a spell while the moon is full for best results. The full moon's bright glow can also put you in the spotlight or shed light on murky issues. If your goal is to attract attention, the full moon helps illuminate you favorably. The full moon can also shine light on secrets and deception to let you get to the truth of a shady situation.

The waning moon—the two weeks after the full moon and before the new moon—encourages decrease. Do you intend to lose weight? Cut expenditures of cash or energy? Cast your spell while the moon is diminishing in size to diminish the impact of something in your life.

YOUR MAGICKAL GUIDE TO ASTROLOGY

As the sun and moon traverse the sky, they move through the twelve constellations of the zodiac. The sun spends about a month in each sign and takes a year to complete its trip through the zodiac. The moon stays in a sign for about two and a half days, traveling through the entire zodiac each month.

Each sign resonates with special energies that you can tap to intensify your spells. For instance, Taurus is the sign of fruitfulness and physical resources. Therefore, spells that involve money or any kind of abundance will be enhanced if you perform them when the sun and/or moon is in Taurus. The following table lists the periods when the sun is positioned in the various zodiac signs, along with the types of spells that are best to do during those times.

SIGN	DATES	DO SPELLS FOR
Aries	3/21—4/19	Competition, courage, vitality, male virility, action, new ventures
Taurus	4/20—5/20	Money, abundance, fertility, gardening, love, sex, property
Gemini	5/21—6/20	Communication, commerce, short trips, intellectual pursuits
Cancer	6/21—7/22	Domestic matters, children, your home, protection, women's health, fertility, intuition
Leo	7/23—8/22	Creativity, the arts, fame, public image, leadership, children, vitality
Virgo	8/23—9/22	Health/healing, work relationships, gardening, pets
Libra	9/23—10/22	Love, friendship, professional partnerships, social activities, the arts, beauty, joint ventures, legal issues

SIGN	DATES	DO SPELLS FOR
Scorpio	10/23—11/21	Legacies, other people's resources, sex, power, divination, occult knowledge
Sagittarius	11/22—12/21	Long-distance travel, sports, expansion/growth, spiritual pursuits, good luck
Capricorn	12/22—1/19	Protection, business/career issues, financial stability, limitations, binding enemies
Aquarius	1/20—2/18	Change, independence, friendship, group endeavors, air travel, ideals
Pisces	2/19—3/20	Intuition, divination, the arts, sea voyages, hidden enemies, invisibility, imagination

To determine when the moon is in a particular sign, consult an astrological calendar. For best results, note the signs in which the sun and moon are placed when you cast a spell, as well as the moon's phase. Each feature contributes to the spell's power, action, and outcome.

BEWARE MERCURY RETROGRADE

One astrological glitch to remember is Mercury Retrograde. Every four months, for about three weeks at a time, the planet Mercury appears to reverse its direction and move backward in the sky. (Consult an ephemeris to find out when.) During these periods, all sorts of disruptions and mistakes can happen. Computers break down, checks get lost in the mail, flights get delayed, and so on.

Mercury rules communication and thinking, so you can see that casting spells might not be a good idea while the planet is in reverse mode. Under this confusing celestial influence, you might overlook something important or lack clarity regarding your intentions. You may not get the result you desire, or the outcome could take longer to materialize than you'd hoped. However, if your goal is to find something you've lost or to reverse a situation, Mercury's retrograde periods may aid spellcasting. A wandering pet might return or an opportunity you missed out on the first time around could come up for grabs again when Mercury turns retrograde.

THE WHEEL OF THE YEAR

Some practitioners celebrate eight holidays that date back to pre-Christian times as exceptionally powerful times for doing magick. The holidays mark the Earth's yearly cycle and the sun's apparent passage through the heavens. (Note: these dates are based on the sun's position in the sky relative to Earth, and can vary a day or so from year to year.)

HOLIDAY	DATE
Samhain (pronounced SOW-een)/ Halloween/All Hallows' Eve	October 31
Yule/Winter Solstice	December 21
Imbolc/Brigid's Day and Candlemas	February 1
Ostara/Spring Equinox	March 21
Beltane	May 1
Midsummer/Summer Solstice	June 23
Lammas/Lughnasadh	August 1
Mabon/Autumn Equinox	September 22

According to early Earth-honoring traditions, each holiday has a particular meaning. Notice that many of our contemporary holidays bear close connections to these historic ones. You'll find lots of books and websites that explain their meanings and how to celebrate them. Don't hesitate, however, to put your own spin on the festivities and to add your own magick to ancient customs.

WHEN ARE YOUR POWER DAYS?

According to numerology, your birthday is a power day, when your personal energies are at a peak; therefore, it's a good time to do magick. But that's not your only fortunate day—you actually have them all throughout the year. For instance, if you were born on the fourteenth day of a month, then the fourteenth day of every month is lucky for you.

Numerology also teaches that each number possesses a distinct resonance that can aid your spells. The following table lists the single-digit numbers and their magickal meanings.

NUMBER	MEANING
1	Beginnings, individuality
2	Partnership, love, joint ventures
3	Creativity, good fortune, manifestation, to seal a spell
4	Stability, security, protection
5	Change, movement, travel, communication
6	Shared resources, cooperation, beauty, happiness
7	Peace, spiritual growth, retreat, healing
8	Business/career pursuits, financial security, permanence, binding
9	Fulfillment, abundance, growth, luck

Let's say the company you work for is downsizing and you want to protect your job. Good dates to cast a spell are the fourth or the eighth of the month. But what if those dates have already passed and you can't wait until next month? Not to worry. Choose a date with two digits that produce the sum 4 or 8 when added together; for example, the thirteenth (1 + 3 = 4) or the twenty-sixth (2 + 6 = 8).

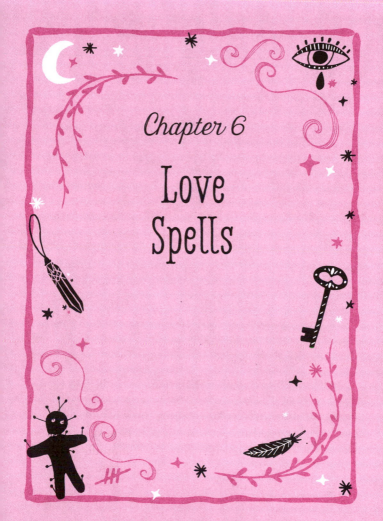

Chapter 6

Love
Spells

It will probably come as no surprise, but some of the most common spells are—you guessed it—love spells. Whether you're looking for something to help smooth over a silly argument, prepare you for the next big steps in your relationship, or even get you noticed by someone you like, you'll find the spells you need here. Love spells can be tricky and can sometimes seem a little questionable. It's easy to let your heart rule your head, so make sure you give yourself time to think about what you really want in a relationship. What are your motives for casting a spell? Do you really want to snag a guy who's not that into you? If your girlfriend is cheating on you, do you really want her back? Don't forget: it's just as important to practice self-love and remember that you deserve only kindness and respect in all of your romantic relationships.

Balm to Reclaim Your Broken Heart

She rejects your love. He finds someone else. There's nothing good about a broken heart. This spell helps you take back your heart by easing the pain of losing the one you love(d).

WHAT YOU NEED

* A piece of rose quartz
* A glass jar or bottle, preferably green, with a lid or stopper
* Mild soap
* Water
* A soft cloth

* 9 ounces of olive, almond, or grape seed oil
* 6 drops of rose, jasmine, or ylang-ylang essential oil
* ¼ teaspoon of dried chamomile leaves

BEST TIME TO PERFORM THE SPELL

Begin on the new moon and continue for as long as necessary

WHAT TO DO

1. Wash the rose quartz and the jar or bottle with mild soap and water, then pat them dry with the soft cloth. Cast a circle around the area where you will do your spell. Pour the olive, almond, or grape seed oil into the jar. Add the essential oil and inhale the fragrance, allowing it to relax your mind. Crush the chamomile leaves very fine and sprinkle them in the oil. Add the rose quartz.

2. Cap the jar and shake it three times to blend and charge the ingredients. Open the circle.

3. Before going to bed, pour a little of the magick balm into your palm and dip your index finger in it. Then rub the oil on your skin at your heart center. Feel it gently soothing the pain. Take several slow, deep breaths, inhaling the pleasant scent, letting it calm your thoughts and emotions. Repeat each night and each morning until your sadness diminishes.

Spell 🎼 End an Argument

You've had an argument, and all you're feeling right now is frustrated, hurt, and angry. Those tricky feelings might be keeping you from making up, so try this spell to help bring you back together peacefully.

WHAT YOU NEED

* A clear quartz crystal
* Mild soap
* Water
* A soft cloth
* A ballpoint pen
* A piece of paper
* Jasmine essential oil
* 2 pink candles
* 2 candleholders
* Matches or a lighter

BEST TIME TO PERFORM THE SPELL

As soon as possible

WHAT TO DO

1. Wash the quartz crystal with mild soap and water, then pat it dry with the soft cloth. Cast a circle around the area where you will do your spell. On the piece of paper write down everything you like and enjoy about your partner. When you've finished, put a drop of essential oil on each corner of the paper and fold it three times.

2. Use the ballpoint pen to inscribe your name on one of the candles and your beloved's name on the other. Dress the candles by rubbing a little essential oil on them (not on the wicks). Fit the candles in their holders and position them on your altar, a table, or other flat surface, so they are about a foot apart. Lay the folded piece of paper between the candles and set the crystal on top of the paper. Light the candles.

3. Close your eyes and bring to mind an image of your partner. Say to that image: "I honor the Divine within you. I forgive you and I forgive myself. I am grateful for the good times we've known together. I bless you and love you. Namaste." Let go of anger, resentment, recrimination, criticism, and so forth that you have held toward your partner. When you're ready, open your eyes and snuff out the candles. Open the circle.

4. If necessary, repeat the spell the next day, only this time move the two candles a little closer together. Do this spell daily, moving the candles closer each time, until you've mended the rift between you.

Spell 🔄 Get You Noticed

Does it sometimes seem like you're invisible? If you aren't getting the attention you seek, it's time to boost your personal power! This spell helps you raise energy and project it into your environment, so that other people will notice you.

WHAT YOU NEED

- ★ A clear quartz crystal
- ★ Mild soap
- ★ Water
- ★ A soft cloth
- ★ A drum or gong

BEST TIME TO PERFORM THE SPELL
During the full moon

WHAT TO DO

1. Wash the quartz crystal with mild soap and water, then pat it dry with the soft cloth. Cast a circle around the area where you will do your spell. Stand or sit in the center of the circle with the drum or gong. Place the crystal nearby.

2. Play the drum or gong. Feel the vibration breaking down the wall around you that prevents people from seeing you clearly. Imagine you are drawing energy up from the Earth, through your feet, into your body. Envision it as a brilliant silver light moving up your legs and spine, until your entire body is filled with a glow.

3. Continue playing the drum or gong as you now imagine drawing energy down from the heavens. Visualize this as golden light flowing into the crown of your head, down your spine, until your whole body is alive with a golden glow. Pick up the crystal and hold it to your heart.

4. Strike the drum or gong one time as you imagine the mixture of silver and gold light radiating outward from your heart. As it flows through the crystal the light is magnified tenfold and spreads out, filling the room. Strike the drum or gong again as you send the light further, into the environment outside. You can project this powerful light as far and wide as you choose.

5. When you feel confident and secure in your new-found radiance, open the circle. Pick up the crystal and carry it with you at all times. It will retain the energy of the spell and continue resonating with it, enhancing your personal power wherever you go.

Spell to Turn Up the Heat

Has the spark gone out of your relationship? Not to worry—this spell uses cayenne pepper and ginger to add some spice right back into your love life. It also lets you play with a little bit of fire to really heat things up between you and your partner.

WHAT YOU NEED

* A fireplace, balefire pit, barbecue grill, hibachi, or other place where you can light a fire safely
* Firewood or charcoal (note: don't burn charcoal indoors)
* Matches or a lighter
* A piece of paper
* A pen that writes red ink
* Cayenne pepper
* Mustard seeds
* Ginger
* Jasmine
* Rosemary
* Bay leaves

BEST TIME TO PERFORM THE SPELL

During the waxing moon, preferably on a Tuesday

WHAT TO DO

1. Cast a circle around the area where you will do your spell. Build a small fire.
2. On the paper, use your red pen to write what you find enticing about your partner and what you desire from them. Be as descriptive and explicit as you like—no one but you will read what you've written. When you've finished, draw the runes *Gebo* (which looks like an X) and *Teiwaz* (which looks like an arrow pointing up) around the edges of the paper. These two symbols represent love and passion, respectively.
3. Place the spices on the paper and fold it to make a packet that contains them. Visualize you and your lover in a passionate embrace. As you hold this image in

your mind, toss the packet into the fire. As it burns, your intention is released into the universe. Open the circle.

Spell to Tie Down a Cheating Partner

Few things hurt as much as being betrayed by the one you love. This spell puts a magick "leash" on your wayward partner so they will stay close to home. A word of warning: by casting this spell you bind your partner to you and vice versa, so be certain that's what you truly want before going ahead. This spell could take some time so feel free to perform it in stages.

WHAT YOU NEED
- ★ Thread
- ★ A needle
- ★ Your partner's underpants (ideally, *all* of the undies)

BEST TIME TO PERFORM THE SPELL
On a Saturday, when the sun or moon is in Taurus

WHAT TO DO
1. Cast a circle. Thread your needle and sew a stitch into the waistband of the first pair of underpants (try to do this so it doesn't show). Tie a knot and say or think this affirmation: "[Name] is faithful to me only, and we are very happy together." Make another stitch, tie a knot, and repeat the affirmation.

2. Continue in this manner until you've sewn a complete circle around the waistband of his or her underpants, with lots of little knots tied along the way. The string of knots, sometimes called a "witch's ladder," holds your intention firmly in place and symbolically ties the two of you together in an exclusive partnership.

3. When you've finished sewing as many garments as you feel up to working on, say aloud: "This spell is done in harmony with Divine Will, our own true wills, and for the good of all, harming none." This disclaimer invites a higher power to take it from here and neutralizes the manipulative aspect of the spell. If, ultimately, the relationship isn't in your best interests, you're giving Divine Will license to act on your behalf to release you from the spell.

4. Open the circle. Repeat the spell as many times as necessary until you've stitched your intention into every pair of your lover's underpants.

Spell to Leave Bad Relationships Behind

You and your partner no longer see eye to eye, and you both know it's time to move on. This spell severs the bond between you, so you can both get on with your individual lives. If you wish—and your soon-to-be-ex agrees—you can enact this spell together to finalize the break.

WHAT YOU NEED

- ★ A fireplace, balefire pit, barbecue grill, hibachi, or other place where you can light a fire safely
- ★ Matches or a lighter
- ★ Firewood or charcoal (note: don't burn charcoal indoors)
- ★ 2 pieces of black cord
- ★ Scissors
- ★ A handful of dried ash leaves

BEST TIME TO PERFORM THE SPELL

During the waning moon, preferably on a Saturday

WHAT TO DO

1. Cast a circle around the area where you will do your spell. Build a small fire.
2. Tie the two pieces of cord together. If you are doing this spell with your partner, give him or her one piece of cord and hold the other piece yourself. Say aloud: "This knot represents the bond between us." With the scissors, cut through the knot, separating the cords again. Say aloud: "The bond between us is now severed. What was two, then one, is now two again."
3. Drop the cords into the fire, then scatter the ash leaves in the flames. Envision the separation between you; see yourself walking away from the relationship alone. Say aloud: "Go in peace [partner's name] and let there be peace between us always. Blessed be." Open the circle.

Amulet ℞ Block Unwanted Attention

Some people just won't take no for answer, no matter how many times you tell them you're not interested. If they won't leave you alone, take a hint from social media and block them...in real life! This amulet helps you repel unwanted attention and establish clear boundaries.

WHAT YOU NEED

* A piece of amber
* A piece of onyx
* Mild soap
* Water
* A soft cloth
* Pine incense
* An incense burner
* Matches or a lighter
* A piece of paper
* A pen that writes black ink
* A black pouch, preferably silk or leather
* Dried basil leaves
* Anise or fennel seeds
* An ash leaf
* A white ribbon
* Salt water

BEST TIME TO PERFORM THE SPELL

During the waning moon, preferably on a Saturday

WHAT TO DO

1. Wash the amber and the onyx with mild soap and water, then pat them dry with the soft cloth. Cast a circle around the area where you will do your spell. Fit the incense in its burner and light it.

79

2. On the paper, draw a sigil that uses the letters in the word *protection* (see Chapter 4). As you work, envision yourself safe and sound, completely surrounded by a sphere of pure white light that no one can penetrate without your permission. When you've finished, draw a circle around the sigil and fold the paper so it's small enough to fit into the pouch. Put the sigil, botanicals, amber, and onyx into the pouch.

3. Tie it closed with the white ribbon, making eight knots. Each time you tie a knot repeat this incantation aloud:

   "From energies I don't invite
   This charm protects me day and night."

4. Sprinkle the amulet with salt water, then hold it in the incense smoke for a few moments to charge it. Open the circle. Wear or carry the amulet with you at all times, until the annoying person stops bothering you.

Lie Detector Serum

Do you suspect your partner isn't telling you the truth? This spell acts as a lie detector and helps you get to the heart of the matter. Instead of administering the truth serum to your partner, you drink it yourself to open your second sight. But there's no going back once you take a sip, so be sure you really want to know what's going on before you drink up...

WHAT YOU NEED

- ★ 6 cups water
- ★ 1 nettle tea bag
- ★ 1 chamomile tea bag
- ★ 1 yarrow tea bag
- ★ A cup
- ★ ½ teaspoon honey
- ★ 1 dark blue candle
- ★ 1 candleholder
- ★ Matches or a lighter
- ★ A scrying tool (a reflective surface, such as a dark mirror, a crystal ball, a large clear quartz crystal, or a dark bowl filled with water)

BEST TIME TO PERFORM THE SPELL

On the night of the full moon

WHAT TO DO

1. Heat the water and add the nettle, chamomile, and yarrow tea bags. Allow to steep for several minutes, then cool. Add honey to sweeten it. Cast a circle around the area where you will do your spell. Sip the tea while you allow your mind to relax and grow receptive.

2. When you've finished the tea, fit the candle in its holder and set it on your altar, a table, or other surface so the candle flame will be at your eye level when you're sitting down. Light the candle and gaze into its flickering flame for a few moments. Set the scrying tool near the candle, so the light reflects in it.

3. Think about your partner and the issue about which you have concerns. When you feel ready to learn the truth, look into the scrying tool and behold your partner's face before you in the reflective surface.

4. Ask whatever you want to know. You might see visions, hear a verbal response, feel a reaction in your body, or merely sense what's true. Trust your intuition.
5. Continue scrying for as long as you wish, asking more questions if you desire. When you've received all the information you seek or can process at present, extinguish the candle and open the circle.

Talisman to Reignite Your Romance

You're starting to think you're losing interest in your partner. You miss the days when your relationship was spontaneous and fun. Get the romance and passion you need with this talisman, which draws upon the energies of gemstones to help rekindle your enthusiasm.

WHAT YOU NEED

* Carnelian beads with holes drilled in them
* Opal beads with holes drilled in them
* Pearls with holes drilled in them
* Moonstone beads with holes drilled in them
* Red coral beads with holes drilled in them
* Mild soap
* Water
* A soft cloth
* Jeweler's wire, enough to make a necklace
* Ylang-ylang or jasmine essential oil

BEST TIME TO PERFORM THE SPELL

During the waxing moon, preferably on a Friday

WHAT TO DO

1. Wash the gemstones with mild soap and water, then pat them dry with the soft cloth. Cast a circle around the area where you will do your spell. Begin stringing the beads on the jeweler's wire. String the stones in any combination, as many of each as you feel you need. Carnelian sparks passion. Opal encourages romance. Pearl promotes harmony. Moonstone makes you more accepting of your lover. Red coral heightens desire.

2. As you work, remember the good times you've enjoyed with your beloved. Concentrate especially on the passionate, romantic, and exciting moments between you.

3. Make the necklace as long as you like. When you've strung all the gemstone beads, dot each bead with a little essential oil. Allow the scent to imprint itself on your subconscious. Open the circle. Wear your magick necklace to reawaken passion in your partnership.

Spell to Redirect a Flirtatious Friend

Is a friend getting a little too friendly with your partner? This spell uses sympathetic magick to convey your message: hands off!

WHAT YOU NEED

* A poppet
* Glue or tape
* A photo of your friend
* A marker to write on the figurine
* A black ribbon
* A box with a lid, big enough to put the figurine in

BEST TIME TO PERFORM THE SPELL

During the waning moon, preferably on a Saturday

WHAT TO DO

1. If possible, create the poppet yourself out of wax, clay, cloth, or wood. If you aren't handy you can purchase a readymade one instead. Cast a circle around the area where you will do your spell. Glue or tape the photo of your friend on the poppet.

2. With the marker write your friend's full name on the poppet. Say aloud: "Figure of [whatever material the poppet is made of], I name you [your friend's name] and command you to keep your hands off [your beloved's name]."

3. Tie the poppet's hands with the black ribbon. Place the poppet in the box and close it.

4. Say aloud: "This spell is cast with love and compassion, harming none. Blessed be."

5. Open the circle. Place the poppet in the friendship sector of your home. To locate this spot, stand at the door you use most often to enter and leave your home, facing in. The friendship sector is to your right.

Talisman ☆ᴵᴼᴿ Next-Level Relationships

Are you having trouble taking the next steps in your relationship? Whether that's having the dreaded "what are we to each other?" talk or planning for a future together, this talisman helps deepen and stabilize the feelings between you and your partner. However, in order to make this spell work you'll act in a way that seems contrary to your intentions: stop pushing for a commitment and give your partner the space he or she needs.

WHAT YOU NEED

* A piece of rose quartz
* A piece of smoky quartz
* A piece of carnelian
* A piece of hematite
* A gold, silver, or copper ring
* Mild soap
* Water
* A soft cloth
* Rose or jasmine incense
* An incense burner
* Matches or a lighter
* A pink or rose silk pouch
* A strand of your hair
* A strand of your partner's hair
* A red ribbon
* Salt water

BEST TIME TO PERFORM THE SPELL

On a Friday during the waxing moon, preferably when the sun and/or moon is in Taurus or Libra

WHAT TO DO

1. Wash the gemstones and the ring with mild soap and water, then pat them dry with the soft cloth.

2. Cast a circle around the area where you will do your spell. Fit the incense in its burner and light it. Put the four stones into the silk pouch. Tie the strands of hair around the ring if they're long enough; if not, simply put the hairs and the ring into the pouch.

3. Close the pouch with the red ribbon, tying eight knots. As you tie each knot, repeat this incantation:
   "I love you and you love me
   Together we shall always be
   And live in perfect harmony."

4. When you've finished, sprinkle the talisman with salt water then hold it in the incense smoke for a few moments to charge your charm. Say aloud: "This is done in harmony with Divine Will, our own true wills, and for the good of all."

5. Open the circle. Place the talisman in the relationship sector of your bedroom. To locate this spot, stand at the entrance to your bedroom, facing in. The relationship sector is the rear right-hand corner.

Lotion FOR Maximum Spark

Are you missing the passion and happiness in your relationship lately? This lotion stimulates the senses to create loving feelings between you and your partner and deepen your connection to one another.

WHAT YOU NEED

* A copper bowl
* A silver or silver-plated spoon
* A glass or china container with a lid (ideally the container should be pink or red, and/or decorated with designs that represent love to you, such as roses or hearts)
* Mild soap
* Water
* A soft cloth
* Unscented massage oil or lotion
* Essential oils of rose, jasmine, ylang-ylang, patchouli, and/or musk (Choose the scents you like: one, two, or all of them. If you choose to use three or more essential oils, you may only add 1–2 drops of each, while you may use 5–6 if you select only one oil.)

BEST TIME TO PERFORM THE SPELL

During the waxing moon, preferably on a Friday

WHAT TO DO

1. Wash the bowl, spoon, and container with mild soap and water, then pat them dry with the soft cloth. Cast a circle around the area where you will do your spell.
2. Pour the massage oil or lotion into the copper bowl. Add a few drops of one of the essential oils you've chosen.

3. Using the silver spoon, stir the mixture making three clockwise circles. Add a few drops of the second essential oil (if you've opted to include more than one).

4. Again, make three clockwise circles to stir the blend. Repeat this process each time you add an essential oil. The more essential oil you add, the stronger the scent will be, so modify the number of drops you add depending on how many scents you choose.

5. As you work, envision a beautiful pink light running from your heart to your partner's heart, growing to envelop you both in its radiant glow. When you've finished, pour the lotion/oil into the glass/china container and put the lid on. Open the circle.

6. Choose a time and place where you and your partner can spend an extended period of time together, undisturbed. Take turns massaging each other with the magick lotion. Relax and engage your senses. Allow the soothing touch and fragrant oils to enhance the connection between you.

Potion ᶠᴼᴿ Extra Romance

Your relationship isn't bad, it's just a little flat—like soda without the bubbles. This spell is designed to pump some romance back into the partnership. Perform it with your partner.

WHAT YOU NEED

- ★ 2 rose-colored candles
- ★ 2 candleholders
- ★ Matches or a lighter
- ★ A chalice
- ★ Sparkling apple cider
- ★ 3 drops of California wild rose flower essence (available at health food stores or online)

BEST TIME TO PERFORM THE SPELL

During the waxing moon, preferably on a Friday or when the sun and/or moon is in Libra

WHAT TO DO

1. Cast a circle around the area where you will do your spell so that both of you are inside the circle. Set the candles on your altar (or a table, mantel, and so forth). Light one yourself and let your lover light the other candle.

2. Pour the cider into your chalice. Add the flower essence. Share the drink, passing the chalice back and forth, while you focus on your desire for one another. When you've finished the drink, extinguish the candles and open the circle.

Spell to Set a Jealous Partner Straight

Your partner overreacts whenever you look at or talk to someone else, even though they know they have no reason to worry. Jealousy and mistrust are driving a wedge between you. This magick spell helps chase away envy and sweetens the situation for you both.

WHAT YOU NEED

* A ballpoint pen
* 1 small pink pillar candle—not a dripless one
* Jasmine essential oil
* A heat-resistant glass, ceramic, or metal plate
* Matches or a lighter
* Dried white rose petals
* Dried nettle

BEST TIME TO PERFORM THE SPELL

During the waning moon, preferably on a Friday, or when the sun and/or moon is in Libra

WHAT TO DO

1. Cast a circle around the area where you will do your spell. With the ballpoint pen, inscribe your partner's name on the candle; the candle represents your partner. Dress the candle by rubbing a little of the jasmine essential oil on it (not on the wick).

2. Set the candle on the plate and light it. Gaze at the candle and imagine you are looking at your partner. Explain your feelings and tell your partner how much you care, how important the relationship is to you. Reassure this person that you are trustworthy. Think only positive thoughts. Allow the candle to burn down completely.

3. While the melted wax is still warm, crumble the rose petals and the dried nettle. Sprinkle the botanicals on the wax. Then form the soft wax into the shape of a heart. Open the circle and give the wax heart to your partner as a token of your affection and fidelity.

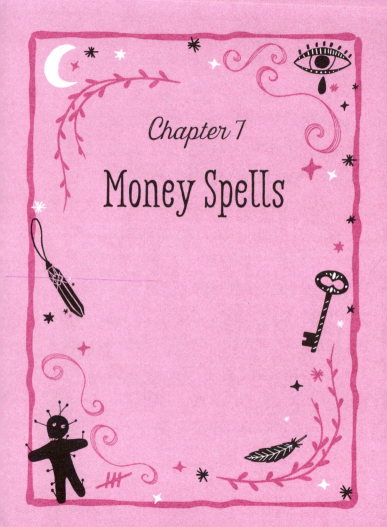

Chapter 7

Money Spells

It's that dreaded time of the month—time to pay bills, that is. Maybe you're paying off a car loan or trying to buy another week's worth of groceries. Maybe your intimidating student loan debt is already staring you down. Or maybe you're just in need of a little fun, like a night out with friends, a fancy dinner with your partner, or even a plane ticket to someplace exotic. You've already tried cutting back on your beloved morning coffee and other so-called unnecessary expenses *and* working out a budget that makes sense, but those bills keep right on rolling in. So what's a witch to do? When the going gets tough, just conjure up a little cash to get you through. Whether you're just trying to pay your bills or want a little extra for something special, magick can help.

Spell ⚗ Stop Dreading Bills

The key to this spell's success is simple—just stop dreading those bills! Easier said than done perhaps, but this spell helps give you the attitude shift you need. Remember that your creditors have provided goods or services up front because they're confident you'll be able to pay. Now it's time for you to believe in yourself!

WHAT YOU NEED

- A piece of green paper or paper designed to resemble money
- Scissors
- A pen that writes gold or silver ink
- All bills that are due
- Checkbook
- A black ribbon
- Peppermint incense
- An incense burner
- Matches or a lighter

BEST TIME TO PERFORM THE SPELL
Whenever you pay your bills

WHAT TO DO

1. Cast a circle around the area where you will do your spell. Use the scissors to cut the green paper into a rectangle the size and shape of paper currency and write *One Million Dollars* on it. Use the pen with gold or silver ink to write the following affirmation on the green paper: "I always have enough money to pay my bills. My prosperity increases every day in every way."

2. After you've finished writing checks to cover your bills, stack the receipts and place the piece of green paper on top of them. Tie everything up with the black ribbon. Fit the incense in its burner and light it. Hold the envelopes containing your checks in the smoke for a few moments. Put aside any fears and imagine you have everything you need, when you need it. Open the circle. Repeat this spell every time you pay your bills.

Spell to Cover Unexpected Expenses

When you least expect it, often at the most inopportune time, something goes wrong. Your car's air conditioner dies suddenly, or you drop your phone and crack the screen beyond use. Don't let yourself to get too stressed out about it—here's the spell you need to generate extra cash to cover those emergency expenses.

WHAT YOU NEED

* A ballpoint pen
* 1 green candle
* 1 gold candle
* 1 silver candle
* 3 candleholders
* Enough coins to form a circle around all three candles (any denomination)
* Matches or a lighter

BEST TIME TO PERFORM THE SPELL

Preferably during the waxing moon, but in an emergency, you can do this spell as necessary

WHAT TO DO

1. Cast a circle around the area where you will do your spell. Using the ballpoint pen, carve the word *money* on the green candle. Inscribe the gold candle with the word *abundance* and write *now* on the silver candle. Set the candles in the candleholders on your altar or another place where they can burn safely. Position them so they form a triangle, with the green and gold candles at the base and the silver one at the apex of the triangle.

2. Next, make a circle around the candles with the coins. Be sure all the coins are face up and that each coin touches those on either side of it. Light the candles and call upon your favorite spiritual helper—a guardian angel, totem animal, or other deity—and ask for assistance in acquiring the money you need.

3. Allow the candles to burn down completely, but don't leave the burning candles unattended. If you must leave the circle before the candles finish burning, extinguish them and continue the spell later. When the candles have burned completely, open the circle and thank the deity for helping you.

Spell FOR When You've Gotta Have It

Whether you've got your eye on a pair of awesome shoes, a brand-new computer, or anything else that's a little bit of a splurge for you, this spell helps get you one step closer to whatever your heart desires. You can magically manifest big things as easily as little ones. The only limits are in your own mind.

WHAT YOU NEED

- ★ A clear quartz crystal or an "abundance" crystal (one that contains a greenish mineral called chlorite)
- ★ Mild soap
- ★ Water
- ★ A soft cloth
- ★ A picture or other likeness of the object you've "gotta have"
- ★ Cedar essential oil

BEST TIME TO PERFORM THE SPELL

During the waxing moon, preferably on a Thursday

WHAT TO DO

1. Wash the crystal with mild soap and water, then pat it dry with the soft cloth. Cast a circle around the area where you will do your spell. Hold the crystal in your left hand while you gaze at the picture of the item you've "gotta have" and imagine yourself already owning it. Involve feelings and senses in the visualization—the more vivid you make the experience the better.

2. When your mind starts to drift, dab each corner of the picture with the cedar essential oil. Let the scent reinforce your intention to acquire the object you desire. When you feel confident that you'll receive your heart's desire, open the circle. Place the picture on your altar, desk, or another place where you'll see it often. Set the crystal on top of the picture to increase the power of your spell. Look at the picture regularly, reaffirming your intention, until the object materializes.

Potion ⚗ Get Cash Quickly

You need cash and you need it now. The good news is, this magick potion starts working as soon as you drink it. You can either brew this potion as a hot tea or enjoy it as a cool drink. If you like, share it with someone else whose intention to get fast cash is linked with your own.

WHAT YOU NEED

* A sharp knife
* ½ teaspoon fresh ginger root
* 2 tablespoons fresh mint leaves
* 2 cups spring water
* Dash cinnamon
* A clear glass or cup (no designs)
* The ace of diamonds from a deck of playing cards

BEST TIME TO PERFORM THE SPELL

During the waxing moon, preferably on a Thursday, but in an emergency, do the spell as necessary

WHAT TO DO

1. Cast a circle around the area where you will do your spell. With the knife, chop the ginger and mint leaves very fine. Sprinkle them in the spring water, then add a dash of cinnamon. If you wish, heat the water to make a tea (but don't let it boil). Pour the herb water in a clear glass or cup.

2. Lay the card face up on your altar, table, or counter-top and set the glass of water on top of it. Leave it for 5 minutes to allow the image on the card to imprint the water with its vibrations. Drink the water. Open the circle. Repeat the spell daily until the cash arrives.

Spell ⚷ Rein in Spending

Does money seem to be going out faster than it's coming in? This spell taps the magick of feng shui to slow your cash outflow and help you get a handle on spending.

WHAT YOU NEED

- ★ A piece of tumbled hematite
- ★ A piece of onyx
- ★ A large stone (one that weighs a pound or two)
- ★ Mild soap
- ★ Water
- ★ A soft cloth
- ★ Your credit cards
- ★ A black envelope
- ★ Pine essential oil
- ★ Your wallet or purse

BEST TIME TO PERFORM THE SPELL

During the waning moon, preferably on a Saturday

WHAT TO DO

1. Wash the stones with mild soap and water, then pat them dry with a soft cloth. Cast a circle around the area where you will do your spell. Sort your credit cards and place the ones you don't need or use regularly—as many as possible—in the black envelope.

2. Next, dab a little of the pine essential oil on each of the stones. When the oil dries, slip the hematite in your wallet or purse—each time you reach for your cash, touch the stone to remind you of your intention. Open the circle.

3. Stash the envelope in a safe spot and set the piece of onyx on it to symbolically hold down spending. Finally, place the large stone in the wealth sector of your home. To locate this, stand at the entrance (the one you use most often, not necessarily the front door) with your back to the door so you're looking inside. The rear left-hand corner is the wealth sector.

Spell FOR When Your Wallet Disappears

You reach for your wallet and realize it's not there. But before you panic and let your imagination run wild, stop and perform this quick and easy spell.

WHAT YOU NEED

★ Nothing but yourself

BEST TIME TO PERFORM THE SPELL

As needed

WHAT TO DO

1. Close your eyes, take a few slow, deep breaths, and calm yourself. In your mind's eye see your wallet (or purse) clearly. Now visualize a ball of pure white light completely surrounding your wallet, encasing it safely inside. Imagine your money, credit cards, driver's license, and so on tucked securely in place.

2. Say or think the following affirmation: "My wallet and its contents are safe and sound. They are returned to me now." You may also wish to ask your favorite deity to help you locate the lost wallet or to intervene if it's been stolen. (Of course, you'll want to notify credit card companies and authorities promptly, especially if your wallet could have been missing for a while and you only just realized it.)

Prosperity Circle to Keep the Money Coming

Your savings account is looking pretty good right now... but you can't predict what the future will bring. This spell ensures that you'll always have more than enough money to cover your expenses.

WHAT YOU NEED

- ★ 9 small jars (baby food jars are perfect)
- ★ A pen that writes green, gold, or silver ink
- ★ A piece of paper
- ★ Coins (any denomination)

BEST TIME TO PERFORM THE SPELL
Daily, beginning during the waxing moon

WHAT TO DO

1. Choose a spot in your home or workplace where you can leave the jars in position permanently, where they won't be disturbed. Cast a circle around the area where you will do your spell. Arrange the empty jars in a circle. Using the colored pen, write the following affirmation on your paper: "I now have plenty of money for everything I need and desire and plenty to share with others." Lay the paper in the center of the circle of jars and put a coin on top to secure it. Then beginning at the east, work in a clockwise direction and drop one coin in each jar. Repeat the affirmation aloud each time you place a coin in a jar. Open the circle.

2. The next day add another coin to each jar, again starting at the east and working in a clockwise direction. Continue in this manner, adding one coin per day to each jar.

3. When all the jars are full, remove the coins and donate the money to your favorite charity.

4. As you give the money away, repeat three times: "I offer this money with love and gratitude. I now receive my tenfold return, with good to all concerned." Start filling the jars again. Continue performing this spell and sharing your wealth indefinitely, in order to keep prosperity coming your way forever.

Oil 🜂 Attract the Good Life

This magick potion can be used alone or mixed with other spells. Dress candles with it. Dab it on talismans or sigils. Anoint gemstones, crystals, or magick tools with it. If you use body-safe glitter, you can rub a little on your body. However you use it, this oil helps you attract all forms of abundance.

WHAT YOU NEED

- A green glass bottle with a lid or stopper
- A piece of tiger's eye or aventurine
- Mild soap
- Water
- A soft cloth

- 4 ounces of olive, almond, or grape seed oil
- 3 drops of peppermint essential oil
- Gold or silver glitter

BEST TIME TO PERFORM THE SPELL

During the waxing moon, preferably on a Thursday

WHAT TO DO

1. Wash the bottle and gemstone with mild soap and water, then pat them dry with the soft cloth. Cast a circle around the area where you will do your spell. Pour the olive, almond, or grape seed oil into the bottle. Add the peppermint essential oil and glitter. Drop the tiger's eye or aventurine in the mixture, then put the lid or stopper on the bottle and shake three times to charge the potion.

2. Open the circle and apply your oil in whatever manner you choose. You can rub it directly on your body, dress candles with it, dab it on crystals and gemstones, or use it to anoint talismans. In fact, this magick oil can be incorporated into most of the spells in this chapter.

Spell ᶠᴏʀ Your Own "Buried Treasure"

No hunting for a hidden pirate's chest for you! In this spell, you're doing the hiding. By symbolically stashing treasure, you'll "prime the pump" so greater riches can flow to you.

WHAT YOU NEED

- ★ A small mirror
- ★ A tin box with a lid
- ★ 9 coins
- ★ A magnet
- ★ A shovel

BEST TIME TO PERFORM THE SPELL
During the waxing moon, preferably on a Thursday

WHAT TO DO
1. Begin by casting a circle around the area where you will do your spell. Place the mirror in the bottom of the tin box, with the reflective side up. Lay the coins, one at a time, on top of the mirror while you envision each one multiplying exponentially. Attach the magnet to the inside of the box (on the lid or a side) and visualize it attracting a multitude of coins to you. Put the lid on the box and open the circle.

2. Take your "treasure chest" and the shovel outside and dig a hole beneath a large tree. Bury the box in the ground near the tree's roots. When you've finished, say this incantation aloud:

"By the luck of three times three
This spell now brings great wealth to me.
The magnet draws prosperity.
The mirror doubles all it sees.
My fortune grows as does this tree
And I shall ever blessed be."

Spell to Make a Money Tree

Money may not grow on trees, but this spell will help you tap into the tree's natural growth symbolism to increase your income.

WHAT YOU NEED
* Gold and/or silver ribbons
* Small charms, earrings, beads, and/or crystals
* Bells or wind chimes

BEST TIME TO PERFORM THE SPELL
During the waxing moon, preferably in the spring or summer; in the fall or winter, do the spell when the waxing moon is in Taurus

WHAT TO DO

1. Tie the ribbons loosely on the branches of a favorite tree that's special to you. Hang the other adornments on the branches as well. These objects represent gifts or offerings to the nature spirits, in return for their assistance in bringing you wealth.

2. As you attach each item, state your intention aloud and ask the nature spirits to help you acquire what you desire. When you've finished, thank the tree and the nature spirits.

Spell to Attract Elemental Money

You've heard of leprechauns, who are said to possess pots of gold. These mythical characters are based on the earth elementals known as gnomes. If you're nice to them, they'll help you acquire your own pot of gold.

WHAT YOU NEED

★ **Chocolate mint cookies**   ★ **A cauldron or bowl**

BEST TIME TO PERFORM THE SPELL

During the waxing moon, preferably when the sun and/or moon is in Taurus

WHAT TO DO

1. Bake or buy chocolate mint cookies. Put a few cookies in your cauldron or bowl and take them outside to a place in nature.

2. Set the cauldron under a bush or at the foot of a tree. Call to the gnomes and tell them you've brought them a gift. Explain that you need money and you know they can help you acquire the wealth you desire. Ask for their assistance and thank them in advance for helping you. Treat them with respect, just as you would a person whose aid you were soliciting.

3. In a day or so, return to the spot with more cookies. Put the cookies in the cauldron or bowl and call to the gnomes again. Do the same thing a day or so later, leaving the cookies and the cauldron under the tree. Soon you may notice money, valuables, or financial opportunities coming into your life, perhaps in unexpected ways. Repeat the spell as needed to keep the flow of wealth coming your way.

Spell to Clear the Way for Wealth

So many expenses, so little money to pay them with. This spell utilizes the ancient Chinese form of magick known as feng shui to clear the way for prosperity and financial success to enter your life.

WHAT YOU NEED
★ **Sage incense**

BEST TIME TO PERFORM THE SPELL
Any time

WHAT TO DO

1. Stand at the door through which you usually enter and leave your home (it may not be your front door) and face in. From this vantage point, locate the section at the rear left-hand corner of your home (you might not actually be able to see it because walls may obscure your vision). This is the area known as your wealth sector and its condition symbolizes your financial condition.

2. Go to this part of your home and visually assess it. Be objective. Is it neat, clean, and orderly? Or cluttered and disorganized? Are there things in this area that you no longer use? Chances are this space could do with a little improvement.

3. Begin by clearing away anything you don't need or use: furniture, clothes, books, CDs, electrical equipment, old paperwork, etc. Repair or get rid of broken, worn, or nonfunctioning items. As long as your wealth sector is cluttered with old stuff, new money can't come in. It may take a while, and you might have to do this in stages. Keep your objective in mind while you work.

4. When you've finished uncluttering your space, neatly organize what remains. While you're at it, give the area a good cleaning. Then smudge the space with sage incense to clear it energy-wise.

Spell ✢ Become a Millionaire

You probably don't believe you can become a millionaire, do you? Maybe that's why you haven't already done it! This spell starts reprogramming your subconscious to believe you can attract a million dollars—and more importantly, to believe that you deserve it.

WHAT YOU NEED

* A likeness of a $1,000,000 bill
* A clear quartz crystal or an "abundance" crystal
* Mild soap
* Water
* A soft cloth

BEST TIME TO PERFORM THE SPELL

During the waxing moon

WHAT TO DO

1. Find a likeness of a $1,000,000 bill. You can download an image from the Internet or simply cut a piece of paper the size and shape of a bill, then write *One Million Dollars* on it. If you wish, add other images to make the bill look as realistic as possible.

2. Place the million-dollar bill face up on your desk, your altar, or in the wealth sector of your home. To locate this, stand at the entrance to your home (the one you use most often, not necessarily the front door) with your back to the door so you're looking inside. The rear left-hand corner is the wealth sector.

3. Wash the crystal with mild soap and water, pat it dry with the soft cloth, then set it on top of the bill.

4. Several times each day, pick up the bill and stare at it as you recite the following affirmation: "I now have $1,000,000 free and clear, to do with as I please. This money comes to me in harmony with Divine Will, my own true will, and for the good of all, harming none. I deserve this money and I accept it thankfully."

5. You don't have to know how the money will come to you, all you have to do is believe it is already on its way. Repeat this spell until you succeed.

Spell to "Mint" Your Own Money

Wouldn't it be nice if you could mint your own money? Well, now you can! No, we're not talking about counterfeiting. Instead, use magick to make your wealth grow.

WHAT YOU NEED

* A likeness of a $1,000,000 bill
* A green ceramic flowerpot
* Potting soil
* Spearmint or peppermint seeds, or a small mint plant
* Water

BEST TIME TO PERFORM THE SPELL

During the waxing moon, preferably when the sun or moon is in Taurus

WHAT TO DO

1. Find a likeness of a $1,000,000 bill. You can download an image from the Internet or simply cut a piece of paper to the size and shape of a bill, then write *One Million Dollars* on it. If you wish, add other images to make the bill look as realistic as possible.

2. Cast a circle around the area where you will do your spell. Fold the bill three times and place it in the bottom of the ceramic flowerpot. Fill the pot with soil. Plant the seeds or seedling in the soil and water it.

3. As you work, repeat this incantation:

   "Every day
   In every way
   Prosperity
   Now comes to me."

4. When you've finished, open the circle. Set the flowerpot in a spot where light and other conditions are favorable. Continue caring for your mint plant and remember to recite the incantation daily. When you trim the plant, save the leaves and dry them to use in talismans. As the plant grows, so will your finances.

Spell ᶠᴼᴿ an Attitude of Gratitude

Your finances don't look good and you can't see any relief on the horizon. However, worrying about the problem will only make it worse. This spell works by shifting your attitude from one of lack to one of abundance.

WHAT YOU NEED

* A notebook or journal
* A pen that writes green ink

BEST TIME TO PERFORM THE SPELL

Every day

WHAT TO DO

1. Each morning, begin the day by writing at least one thing you are thankful for in a notebook or journal with your green pen. It might be good health; it might be a loving family. It could be something nice that happened to you the previous day, such as receiving a phone call from an old friend or getting a bargain at the supermarket.

2. Each night, read some or all of your entries. Pretty soon you'll notice your thinking is beginning to change. You no longer entertain a poverty consciousness. Instead, you see yourself as rich in many ways. Because like attracts like, that sense of abundance will draw more prosperity to you.

Chapter 8

Work
Spells

Whether you're on the hunt for that elusive dream job, starting to climb the corporate ladder, or just punching the clock until something better comes along, the workday is full of challenges. It can be tough to get through the day when it seems like everyone from your coworkers to your customers is conspiring against you. Good thing you're tougher! Use the spells in this chapter to change your day around and make even that lonely late-night shift seem totally manageable. With magick on your side, you can make that dream job seem less like fantasy and more like something you can actually achieve. But make sure to take some time to think about what you really want from your career. Clearly defined needs and expectations will help you attract the work you love.

Spell 🜨 Get the Respect You Deserve

Does your boss overlook your hard work and fail to give you credit for your contributions? Do customers seem unappreciative when you go the extra mile for them? If you're feeling dissed lately, this spell can help you get the respect you deserve.

WHAT YOU NEED

* A ballpoint pen
* 1 orange candle
* Cinnamon essential oil
* 1 candleholder
* Dried bay leaves
* Matches or a lighter
* Colored pens, pencils, or markers
* A piece of paper
* Invisible tape

BEST TIME TO PERFORM THE SPELL

During the full moon, on a Sunday, or when the sun or moon is in Leo

WHAT TO DO

1. Cast a circle around the area where you will do your spell. With the ballpoint pen, inscribe a circle with a dot in its center on the candle; this is the astrological symbol for the sun. Dress the candle by rubbing a little of the essential oil on it (not on the wick) and set it in its holder. Inhale the scent of cinnamon, letting it stimulate feelings of confidence and power. Lay the bay leaves around the base of the candle so they encircle it. Light the candle.

2. With the colored markers and paper, create a sigil from the word *respect* (see Chapter 4). If you like, add other images that represent status, honor, and authority to you. While you work, imagine yourself being lauded by the people you work with. See them bowing down to you, offering you gifts, or singing your praises. When you're happy with your design, put a dot of cinnamon oil on each corner of the piece of paper. Extinguish the candle and collect the bay leaves. Open the circle.

3. Take the sigil and the bay leaves to your workplace. Tape the bay leaves, which represent victory and success, on your desk, computer, door, wall, or other spot in your work area; if you prefer, put them in a desk drawer or other safe place. Display the sigil where you'll see it often. Any time someone behaves disrespectfully toward you, look at the sigil and take a few deep breaths, inhaling self-confidence. Remember Eleanor Roosevelt's words: "No one can make you feel inferior without your consent."

Spell 𝄢ᴏʀ a Bitchy Coworker

There's one at every job—the coworker who makes everyone else's life miserable. The word teamwork isn't in his vocabulary. Her pessimism drags down the rest of the staff's morale. Can a little magick sweeten this sour situation? Absolutely!

WHAT YOU NEED

* A piece of tumbled rose quartz
* A piece of watermelon tourmaline
* Mild soap
* Water
* A soft cloth
* A spray bottle
* Spring water
* Granulated sugar
* Jasmine essential oil
* Lavender essential oil

BEST TIME TO PERFORM THE SPELL

During the waning moon, preferably on a Friday

WHAT TO DO

1. Wash the gemstones with mild soap and water, then pat them dry with the soft cloth. Cast a circle around the area where you will do your spell. Fill the bottle with spring water, then add the sugar and essential oils. Shake the bottle three times to charge the mixture.
2. Envision the annoying coworker encased in a sphere of pink light. Even though this person may be as prickly as a cactus, try to accept that negative people are filled with fear. This spell works by enhancing your coworker's self-esteem, so projecting positive energy will actually defuse this person's bitchiness. Open the circle.
3. Take the magick potion and the gemstones to work with you. When your irritating coworker isn't around, mist their workspace with the water and oil mixture. Repeat as necessary.

4. Place the piece of tournamline in a secret spot somewhere in the bitchy person's work area. (Tourmaline neutralizes and disperses negative energy.) Keep the rose quartz for yourself. Whenever you start feeling annoyed, rub the stone until you calm down. Before long you should notice an improvement in your coworker's attitude and behavior, and in your own reactions to him or her.

Spell to Get a Raise

You work hard at your job, are a team player, and feel like you're exceeding expectations and making a difference. So how do you make sure your salary is what you deserve? This spell uses growth symbolism to help you get a raise.

WHAT YOU NEED

* A clear glass bottle (no designs) with a lid or stopper
* Spring water
* A $20 bill
* Invisible tape

BEST TIME TO PERFORM THE SPELL
During the waxing moon, preferably on a Thursday

WHAT TO DO
1. Cast a circle around the area where you will do your spell. Fill the bottle with spring water. Tape the $20 bill on the side of the bottle. This infuses the water

with the image of money. Cap the bottle and shake it three times to charge it.

2. Drink some of the imprinted water. As you do this, imagine you are being "watered" with wealth. You are actually incorporating prosperity into your body and your consciousness. See your boss calling you into their office and offering you a raise, or envision yourself receiving a paycheck with a larger amount printed on it—choose an image that clearly expresses your intention. Open the circle. Continue drinking your "money water" daily—make more when you finish the first batch—and watch your income increase.

Spell 𝕥𝕠 Attract Your Dream Job

You want to tell your boss to take this job and shove it, but times are tough and good jobs are hard to find. Instead, put your magick skills to work and get busy creating the perfect job for you.

WHAT YOU NEED

- ★ Pictures from magazines, the Internet, or other sources
- ★ A large piece of paper or cardboard
- ★ An orange marker
- ★ Glue, paste, or tape

BEST TIME TO PERFORM THE SPELL

During the waxing moon, preferably on a Sunday or Thursday

WHAT TO DO

1. Spend some time thinking about the job you'd really like. What images do you associate with it? Is travel a factor? If so, a plane might be a good symbol. Perhaps a big walnut desk represents authority to you, or a TV screen suggests fame. Coins and paper currency signify money. Cut out magazine pictures that depict the various facets of your dream job or download images from the Internet.

2. Once you've gathered all your images, cast a circle around the area where you will do your spell. On the paper or cardboard, use the marker to draw a symbol that astrologers call the Part of Fortune. This lucky design looks like an X with a circle around it. Make your drawing large enough so you can paste all your pictures inside its quadrants (if necessary, tape two or more sheets together). Begin gluing or taping the pictures you've collected to the four sectors of the Part of Fortune. As you work, imagine yourself happy and successful in your new position.

3. When you've finished, lay the paper or cardboard on the floor. Remove your shoes and stand in the middle of it. Close your eyes and imagine yourself becoming one with your new job. Make the visualization as real as possible. Stand there until your mind starts to wander, then step off the paper or cardboard and open the circle. Repeat as necessary, until you land your ideal job.

Spell to Wind Down from the Workday

No matter how hard you work, you never seem to get caught up. With constant questions and requests from customers and coworkers, you never seem to get a moment to just breathe. If stress and frustration are getting you down, this spell offers a welcome respite from workplace demands.

WHAT YOU NEED

- ★ Lavender incense
- ★ An incense burner
- ★ 1 light blue candle
- ★ 1 candleholder
- ★ Matches or a lighter
- ★ A bathtub
- ★ Vanilla essential oil
- ★ 4 good-sized chunks of amethyst
- ★ Mild soap
- ★ Water
- ★ A soft cloth

BEST TIME TO PERFORM THE SPELL
Any time

WHAT TO DO

1. Cast a circle around your bathroom. Fit the incense and candle in their respective holders, then light both. Fill the bathtub with pleasantly hot water. Add a little of the vanilla essential oil to the bathwater.

2. Wash the amethysts with mild soap and water, pat them dry with the soft cloth, and then set one on each corner of the bathtub. Climb into the tub and make yourself comfy.

3. Feel the amethysts drawing off your stress and neutralizing it. Feel your frustrations and anxieties dissolving into the bathwater. The trick is not to think about anything outside the walls of the bathroom. When you worry about the past or future, you block receptivity to new ideas and guidance that could help you resolve problems. If a troublesome thought pops into your mind, send it into the water or give it to the amethysts. Soak for as long as you like until you feel calm, rested, and confident that all is well.

4. When your peace of mind is restored, get out of the tub. As the water drains away, visualize your cares flowing away with it. Pick up the amethysts and thank them. Then wash them with clean water (not the bathwater) and mild soap and pat them dry. Extinguish the candle and incense, or allow them to burn down in a safe place. Open the circle and emerge renewed.

Spell to Bind a Backstabber

He spreads damaging gossip about you at work. She steals your ideas and claims they're hers. It's time to bring out the big guns, magically that is. This spell ties the backstabber's hands and prevents him or her from doing further harm.

WHAT YOU NEED

* **A poppet**
* **A black marker**
* **A strand of black cord**
* **A shovel**
* **A large stone**

BEST TIME TO PERFORM THE SPELL

During the waning moon, preferably on a Saturday

WHAT TO DO

1. If possible, create the poppet yourself out of wax, clay, cloth, or wood. If you aren't handy you can purchase a readymade one instead. Cast a circle around the area where you will do your spell.

2. With the marker write the troublemaker's full name on the poppet. Say aloud: "Figure of [whatever material the poppet is made of], I name you [the backstabber's name] and command you to cease your attacks now. I bind your ill will and render you powerless against me."

3. Wrap the black cord around the figurine several times and tie it, making eight knots. Repeat the last sentence of the affirmation—"I bind your ill will and render you powerless against me"—each time you tie a knot. When you've finished, open the circle.

4. Take the poppet and shovel to a place near your workplace and dig a hole in the ground. If that's not feasible, go to a remote area away from trees or water (and not on your own property). Place the poppet in the hole and cover it with dirt, then put the stone on top of it for good measure.

Spell to Cover Your Butt

You did something you shouldn't have...or didn't do something you should have. This spell throws up a magickal smokescreen around you to prevent other people from noticing your error.

WHAT YOU NEED

- Loose sage leaves
- Sprigs of dried rosemary
- Dried basil leaves
- A large shell, fireproof ceramic bowl, or cauldron
- Matches or a lighter
- A fan made of paper, feathers, or cloth
- A small black box
- Peony seeds

BEST TIME TO PERFORM THE SPELL

The night before the new moon (sooner, if necessary)

WHAT TO DO

1. Cast a circle around the area where you will do your spell. Place the sage, rosemary, and basil in the shell, ceramic bowl, or cauldron. Light the herbs, then blow out the flames leaving the herbs to smoke. Set the shell/bowl/cauldron on the floor or ground (in a place where it can continue burning safely).

2. Remove your clothing. Stand near the smoke and use the fan to bring the smoke toward you. Try to direct the smoke so it touches your whole body, head to foot, on both sides.

3. Inhale the fragrant scent of burning herbs while you imagine you are invisible—you are completely concealed by magick smoke. No one can see you or link you with the mistake that was made.

4. When the herbs have burned and cooled, place the ashes in the black box. Add the peony seeds. Get dressed and open the circle. Carry the box with you at all times, until the whole business blows over and you no longer have any concerns.

Spell to Beat Out the Competition

Have you ever seen animals defend their territory? They usually attack with teeth and claws. This spell takes its cue from them. So if your competition's trying to move into your territory, use this spell to rise above the rest of the pack.

WHAT YOU NEED

* Polymer clay
* A large needle
* Scissors
* Jewelry elastic
* A nonstick baking tray

BEST TIME TO PERFORM THE SPELL

On a Tuesday, or when the sun or moon is in Aries

WHAT TO DO

1. Follow the directions on the package of clay to form lots of pointy teeth and claws, each about an inch or two in length.

2. With the needle, pierce each one at the thicker end, making a hole large enough so the jewelry elastic will fit through it. Arrange the teeth and claws on the baking tray, making sure they don't touch each other. Bake according to instructions on the package.

3. Cut a piece of jewelry elastic long enough to go over your head. When the teeth and claws have cooked and cooled, string them on the jewelry elastic to make a necklace. Tie the elastic in a knot at the back. Wear this warrior's necklace to bolster your own courage, so you can scare off the competition and defend what's yours.

Spell to Kickstart a New Project

You're having a hard time getting a project off the ground. Delays and challenges keep slowing you down. This spell plays on the symbolism of eggs as symbols of birth, life, and fertility to help you make your idea a reality.

WHAT YOU NEED

- A raw egg
- A straight pin or needle
- A bowl
- Water
- Acrylic or watercolor paints
- A small paintbrush

BEST TIME TO PERFORM THE SPELL

On the Spring Equinox or on the new moon

WHAT TO DO

1. Cast a circle around the area where you will do your spell. Carefully poke a hole in each end of the egg with a pin. Holding the egg above the bowl, place your mouth over one hole and gently blow the contents of the egg out through the other hole. When you've finished, rinse out the eggshell and let it dry.
2. Paint symbols and images on the eggshell that represent your project, as well as your objectives. Make sure everything you include has positive connotations for you. While you work, visualize your project moving forward and receiving the support and acclaim you seek. See your goals coming to fruition, your success assured.
3. When you've finished decorating your egg, open the circle. Display the egg in a place where you'll see it often. Each time you look at it, you'll be reminded of your goal and your intention to succeed.

Spell to Protect Your Job

Your job is on the line, for reasons that may or may not be your fault. Worrying only makes matters worse, so use your time and energy productively by casting this spell instead.

WHAT YOU NEED

- 4 white stones
- Mild soap
- Water
- Black paint or a black felt-tip marker with permanent ink

BEST TIME TO PERFORM THE SPELL
Any time

WHAT TO DO

1. Wash the stones with mild soap and water. Allow them to dry in the sun. With the black paint or marker, draw a pentagram on each stone.

2. Put one stone on the floor in each corner of your cubicle, office, or work area to stabilize your position. As you set each stone in place, say or think this affirmation: "My job here is safe and secure, and all is well."

Talisman to Make a Good Impression

You've got to make a good impression, but you feel anxious and uncertain. Whether you're going for a job interview, giving a presentation, or meeting with an important client, this lucky charm helps you shine. Remember, the key to success is believing in yourself.

WHAT YOU NEED

* Sandalwood incense
* An incense burner
* Matches or a lighter
* Red nail polish or red paint and a small brush
* A small stone
* A piece of paper
* A pen
* An orange cloth pouch, preferably silk
* Cedar chips
* Cinnamon
* Dried parsley
* A yellow ribbon
* Salt water

BEST TIME TO PERFORM THE SPELL

On a Sunday, preferably when the sun or moon is in Leo

WHAT TO DO

1. Cast a circle around the area where you will do your spell. Fit the incense in its burner and light it. Use the nail polish or paint to draw the rune *Inguz* (which looks like two X's stacked one on top of the other) on the stone. This rune represents new beginnings, fertility, and great power.

2. While the nail polish or paint is drying, write on the paper what you intend to accomplish. Whom do you wish to impress? What results do you desire from this meeting? As you write your list of objectives, envision yourself already achieving them. When you've finished, fold the paper so it's small enough to fit into the pouch and say aloud: "This is now accomplished in harmony with Divine Will, my own true will, and for the good of all."

3. Put the stone, paper, cedar, cinnamon, and parsley into the pouch. Tie the pouch closed with the ribbon, making three knots. Hold the image of your success in your mind as you tie the knots. Sprinkle the talisman with salt water, then hold it in the incense smoke for a few moments to charge the charm.

4. Open the circle. Carry this talisman in your pocket, purse, or briefcase when you go to your meeting to bring you good luck. Just knowing it's there will increase your self-confidence and help you make a good impression.

Incantation 🔔 Inspire

You really need to come up with some great new ideas, but you just don't feel inspired. Chanting can spark your enthusiasm. Think about how a crowd's cheers raise energy and fire up a team—incantations operate on the same principle.

WHAT YOU NEED
* A piece of paper
* A pen that writes red ink
* A drum, gong, or large bell

BEST TIME TO PERFORM THE SPELL
On a Tuesday during the waxing moon

WHAT TO DO
1. Cast a circle around the area where you will do your spell. On the paper, write a rhyme that conveys your intentions. It should praise you and your abilities with positive statements and imagery. Don't worry about the literary quality of your incantation—no one but you will hear it. The point is to make it upbeat and catchy.

2. When you're satisfied with your rhyme, read it aloud. Then strike the drum, gong, or bell. Repeat the incantation again, and again, sounding the drum/gong/bell each time. If you prefer, you can strike the drum/gong/bell after each line or after each word of the incantation. Feel the sounds stimulating your energy. Feel the blockages within you crumbling. Feel your confidence growing. Continue for as long as you like. When you feel inspired, stop and open the circle.

Spell to Open New Doors

Downsizing, outsourcing, or another situation beyond your control has eliminated your job. You know the saying: when one door closes, another one opens. This spell uses the familiar symbolism to bring new career opportunities your way.

WHAT YOU NEED
* Small bells, one for each door in your home
* 9-inch-long red ribbons, one for each door in your home

BEST TIME TO PERFORM THE SPELL
On the new moon

WHAT TO DO
1. Tie one bell at the end of each ribbon, then tie one ribbon to each door in your home.

2. As you work, envision yourself attracting new career opportunities. If you already know the job you'd like to have, see yourself performing it. Or, let the universe provide a position that's right for you. Each time you tie a ribbon on a doorknob, say the following affirmation aloud: "I now have a job that's perfect for me in every way."

3. As you go through the doors in your home daily, you'll constantly be reminded of your intention. The red ribbons represent good luck. The tinkling bells send your request out into the world. Repeat your affirmation every time you open a door, until you land the job you desire.

Belt FOR Everyday Empowerment

In karate, the belt you wear signifies your level of ability and accomplishment. The belt you create in this spell is not only a badge of success, it actually enhances your personal power. Use it when a work situation challenges you to step up to the plate.

WHAT YOU NEED

* Music that energizes you and that signifies power to you
* A purple cord long enough to circle your waist three times (drapery cord is perfect, but you can use any material you like)

BEST TIME TO PERFORM THE SPELL

During the waxing moon, preferably on a Sunday

WHAT TO DO

1. Cast a circle around the area where you will do your spell. Begin playing the music you've selected. Close your eyes and allow the music to make you feel stronger and more energetic. Let your breathing become deeper.

2. Grasp the purple cord in your hands as you envision yourself drawing up silvery light from the Earth. Feel the light flow up your legs, into your torso, arms, and head. Next, visualize yourself drawing golden light down from the heavens, into the crown of your head. Feel this light flow down into your torso, arms, and legs until your body resonates with it. Imagine these two forces blending harmoniously within you and around you, increasing your vitality, confidence, and personal power.

3. Holding on to this sensation, open your eyes and begin tying knots in the cord. See yourself capturing some of the energy you've raised into each knot you tie. Tie as many knots as you like—just make sure the cord will still fit around your waist. When you're finished tying the knots, wrap the belt around your waist three times and secure it. Open the circle. Wear this "power belt" to help you address the challenges before you. If at any time you need a quick rush of vitality or courage, untie one of the knots and release the energy it holds.

Spell ᴲᴼᴿ a Smooth Commute

Nothing makes the workday seem quite so long as a terrible commute to start and end the day. This spell will clear your way for a smooth ride to and from work.

WHAT YOU NEED

★ **An athame**

BEST TIME TO PERFORM THE SPELL

During the waning moon, preferably when the sun or moon is in Gemini or Sagittarius

WHAT TO DO

1. Cast a circle around the area where you will do your spell. Stand in the center of the circle facing the direction you must travel to get to work. Close your eyes and visualize bumper-to-bumper traffic, construction delays, bad weather, or whatever difficulties you usually face during your commute.

2. Holding the athame in your hand, begin slashing through the obstacles, cleaning a path before you. See yourself zipping along the open road smoothly and easily, until you reach your destination. When you've finished, open the circle. Repeat this spell as needed.

Spell 🜔 to Get Rid of an Annoying Customer

You've done the best you can, but a customer still isn't satisfied. Even worse, they keep bothering you, complaining, demanding more and more. This spell erects an invisible boundary around you to protect you from this troublemaker while simultaneously neutralizing their power.

WHAT YOU NEED

- ★ 8 black candles
- ★ 9 candleholders
- ★ A symbol of you or your company, such as a
- photograph or logo drawn on paper
- ★ 1 red candle
- ★ Matches or a lighter

BEST TIME TO PERFORM THE SPELL

Begin during the waning moon, preferably when the moon is in Capricorn

WHAT TO DO

1. Cast a circle around the area where you will do your spell. Fit the black candles in their holders and arrange them in a tight circle on your altar or another surface where they can remain in place safely for eight days. Set the symbol of you or your company in the middle of the circle of candles. Fit the red candle in its holder and position it several inches away from the circle of black candles—it represents the problem customer. Light all the candles and say this incantation aloud:

"From your complaints
Now [I am][we are] free.
Go far away
And let [me][us] be."

2. As you gaze at the pattern on your altar, visualize your antagonist losing credibility and receding into the distance. After a few minutes, extinguish the candles and open the circle.

3. The next day repeat the ritual. This time, however, move the red candle an inch or two further away from the rest to signify its retreat. Light all the candles and recite the incantation again, while you imagine the annoying client losing ground against you. When you feel ready, extinguish the candles and open the circle.

4. Repeat the ritual in this way for six more days. On the last day, allow the candles to burn down completely. Take any remnants of candle wax and bury them in a spot far away from your home or business.

Spell to Stand Strong

Setbacks, disappointments, losses, or frustrating circumstances make you feel like giving up. Instead, try this spell, which draws upon the fire power of the universe and asks the fire elementals to boost your energy and confidence.

WHAT YOU NEED

* ★ 9 small red votive candles
* ★ Matches or a lighter
* ★ A magick wand

BEST TIME TO PERFORM THE SPELL

During the waxing moon, preferably on a Tuesday or when the sun and/or moon is in Aries, Leo, or Sagittarius

WHAT TO DO

1. Arrange the candles in a circle around you, in a place where you can safely leave them to burn down completely. Beginning in the east, light the candles one at a time as you move in a clockwise direction around the circle. When all the candles are burning, stand in the center of the circle and face south.

2. Call out to the salamanders, the elementals who inhabit the element of fire. Tell them you have lit nine candles in their honor. Explain your situation and request their assistance, by chanting this incantation aloud:

   "Beings of fire
   Shining so bright
   Fuel my desire
   Increase my might.
   Help me be strong
   All the day long
   So in every deed
   I'll surely succeed."

3. You may notice faint flickerings of light—other than the candles—in the room or sense the energy around you quickening. It might even seem a bit warmer. That means the salamanders are present and willing to work with you.

4. Take up your magick wand and point it toward the south. Envision yourself drawing powerful energy in through the tip of your wand. You might see the wand glow or feel it tingle. Now turn the wand and aim it at yourself. Your movements should be strong and purposeful, not wimpy. Sense the energy you've attracted from the south—the region where the salamanders reside—flowing from the wand into your body. Feel yourself growing more powerful, more confident, more alive.

5. Continue using your wand to pull energy and courage from the south in this manner for as long as you like. Remain in the center of the circle of candles until they have all burned down completely. Thank the salamanders for their assistance and leave the circle with renewed vitality and confidence.

Chapter 9

Protection Spells

The world can be a scary place. So let's take a hint from our ancient ancestors and break out some magick to protect ourselves! For everything from safeguarding our homes and belongings to keeping our feelings out of harm's way to protecting our loved ones, both human and animal, these spells will help keep you safe from all the hidden evils of the world. Warning: there may be danger out in the wide and wild world, but it doesn't do anyone good to dwell on it. You already know about the power of the mind, and you can drive yourself crazy worrying about all those bad things that *might* happen, but probably never will. If you don't want something to happen, don't spend time thinking about it!

Spell ✦FOR✦ On-the-Spot Protection

You're out later than expected in a bad part of town. You and your friends are hiking in the mountains and the trail is more treacherous than you'd expected. It's time for some on-the-spot magick! This quick and easy spell can be done anywhere, in any situation, to provide instant protection.

WHAT YOU NEED

★ **Nothing but yourself**

BEST TIME TO PERFORM THE SPELL

Any time

WHAT TO DO

1. Begin breathing slowly and deeply. If possible, close your eyes. Imagine you are in the center of a sphere of pure white light that completely encloses you like a cocoon. Envision the light spinning clockwise around you. See the light expanding, providing a thick wall of protection that extends outward from your body in all directions. If you're in a car, plane, or other vehicle, visualize the white light surrounding the vehicle as well.

2. Say or think this affirmation: "I am surrounded by divine white light. I am safe and sound, protected at all times and in all situations." Repeat the affirmation three times. Feel yourself growing calmer and more confident as you place your welfare in the hands of a higher force.

Amulet for Extra Protection

A dicey situation has you worried and you feel like you could use some extra protection lately. Protection amulets are one of the oldest forms of magick. This one helps to shield you from potential injury or illness.

WHAT YOU NEED

- ★ A piece of amber (for complete protection)
- ★ A piece of bloodstone (for protection from physical injury)
- ★ A piece of turquoise (for protection from illness)
- ★ Mild soap
- ★ Water
- ★ A soft cloth
- ★ Pine incense
- ★ An incense burner
- ★ Matches or a lighter
- ★ A photo of you (or another person if you're doing this spell for someone else)
- ★ A pen that writes black ink
- ★ Rosemary essential oil
- ★ A white pouch, preferably silk
- ★ A black ribbon
- ★ Salt water

BEST TIME TO PERFORM THE SPELL

During the waning moon, preferably on a Saturday

WHAT TO DO

1. Wash the gemstones with mild soap and water, then pat them dry with the soft cloth. Cast a circle around the area where you will do your spell. Fit the incense in its burner and light it.

2. Across the photograph write the words *I am safe* as you envision yourself completely surrounded by a sphere of pure white light. Dot each corner of the photo with the rosemary essential oil. Inhale the scent of the oil and mentally connect it with a feeling of safety. Slip the photo into the pouch; if necessary, fold it so it's small enough to fit.

3. Rub a little essential oil on each of the stones and add them to the pouch. Tie the pouch closed with the black ribbon, making eight knots. Each time you tie a knot repeat this incantation aloud:

"Anything that could cause harm
Is now repelled by this magick charm."

4. Sprinkle the amulet with salt water, then hold it in the incense smoke for a few moments to charge it. Open the circle. Wear or carry the amulet with you at all times to protect you from harm, or give it to the person you wish to protect.

Lotion 🍶 Boost Bravery

You have to do a presentation or attend an interview, and your palms are already sweating at the thought. Instead of worrying, concoct this magick lotion that boosts your courage.

WHAT YOU NEED

- ★ A small carnelian or ruby
- ★ A glass jar or bottle, preferably amber-colored, with a lid or stopper
- ★ Mild soap
- ★ Water
- ★ A soft cloth
- ★ 8 ounces of almond oil
- ★ 3 drops of amber essential oil
- ★ 3 drops of cedar essential oil
- ★ ¼ teaspoon dried basil leaves

BEST TIME TO PERFORM THE SPELL

Several days before your appearance, preferably on a Tuesday or Sunday; if you don't have that much time, do the spell as needed

WHAT TO DO

1. Wash the gemstone and the bottle/jar with mild soap and water, then pat them dry with the soft cloth. Cast a circle around the area where you will do your spell.
2. Pour the almond oil into the bottle/jar. Add the essential oils and inhale the fragrance, allowing it to invigorate your mind. Crumble the basil leaves very fine and add them to the oil. Add the gemstone. Cap the bottle/jar and shake it three times to blend and charge the ingredients. Open the circle.
3. Each morning, pour a little of the magick oil into your palm and dip your index finger in it. Then rub the oil on your skin at your heart center. Feel it strengthening your confidence.

4. Take several slow, deep breaths, letting the scent strengthen and vitalize you. Repeat each morning until your fear diminishes. Rub a little extra on your chest immediately before you must face any potential critics.

Shield FOR a Safe Home

A home in your neighborhood has been broken into or vandalized, and you're concerned that your home could be next. In this spell, you create an energetic shield that protects your home like a magick wall.

WHAT YOU NEED

- A nail file, small knife, or other sharp tool
- 1 black candle
- 1 candleholder
- Matches or a lighter
- Pieces of white paper, one for each door in your home
- A ballpoint pen that writes black ink

BEST TIME TO PERFORM THE SPELL
As needed, but preferably on a Saturday

WHAT TO DO

1. Cast a circle around the area where you will do your spell. Use the nail file or other tool to engrave a pentagram into the candle wax. Fit the candle in its holder and light it.

2. On the piece of paper, draw a sigil that uses the word *protection* (see Chapter 4).

3. As you work, envision your home surrounded by a high wall of pure white light that intruders can't enter or climb. If you like, add symbols, words, or other images that convey safety to you. When you've finished, draw a circle around the design you've created.

4. Drip a bit of melted candle wax on each corner of the paper. Use the nail file or other tool to inscribe a pentagram in the warm wax.

5. Repeat this procedure, until you've made a shield for each door into your home. Extinguish the candle and open the circle. Attach a safety shield to the inside of each door to repel unwanted visitors.

Circle ᴏꜰ Security

This spell is a great way to keep your home safe from harm of any kind—acts of nature as well as human menaces. If you live in a house and have a yard, you'll need enough crystals to completely circle your house. If you live in an apartment, you'll need one crystal for each window and each door.

WHAT YOU NEED

- ★ Small clear quartz crystals
- ★ Mild soap
- ★ Water
- ★ A soft cloth
- ★ Shield for a Safe Home (see previous spell)
- ★ A black cloth
- ★ A bowl or other small container
- ★ A garden trowel or shovel

BEST TIME TO PERFORM THE SPELL
Begin on a Saturday or during the new moon

WHAT TO DO
1. Wash the crystals with mild soap and water, then pat them dry with a soft cloth. If you have a large area to cover and a lot of crystals, you might need to repeat this spell several times.

2. Lay the Shield for a Safe Home on your altar or a table, sigil side up. Place the crystals on it and visualize them absorbing the intention you put into the symbol. Lay the black cloth over the crystals and the Shield for a Safe Home, covering them completely. Allow the crystals to sit overnight.

3. In the morning, remove the cloth. Pick up the crystals and put them in a bowl or other small container. Take the crystals and your shovel or trowel outside. Beginning in the east, bury the crystals in your yard one at a time, making a protective circle that surrounds your home. If you live in an apartment, start at the east and place a crystal on each interior windowsill of your living space. Then set a crystal in a safe spot near or above each door. As you work, repeat this affirmation aloud:
   "Crystals wise, crystals strong
   Protect my home all day long.
   Crystals clear, crystals bright
   Keep it safe throughout the night."

4. When you've finished, reposition your Shield for a Safe Home on your door.

Amulet Against Evil

Since ancient times, people in cultures around the world have used eye amulets to ward off evil of all kinds. Whether the evil force threatening you is human, animal, or supernatural, this all-seeing protection charm guards your home and its inhabitants.

WHAT YOU NEED

* A disc of wood, ceramic, or stone about 1½ inches in diameter
* Blue, black, and white paint
* A small paintbrush
* A white ribbon at least 1 inch wide and 4–6 inches long
* Tacky glue or something to attach the disk to the ribbon
* A small loop or hook for hanging

BEST TIME TO PERFORM THE SPELL
On a Saturday

WHAT TO DO

1. Cast a circle around the area where you will do your spell. Paint a blue eye on the disc—make it realistic or stylized.

2. Decorate the ribbon with symbols or designs that represent protection to you, such as pentagrams or circles.
3. When the paint dries, attach both ends of the ribbon to the back of the disk to form a loop.
4. Open the circle. Affix the loop or hook to the wall near the front door. Loop the ribbon over the hook to hang your amulet. Each time you enter or leave your home, touch the eye amulet for good luck and to reinforce your intention.

Potion 🜂 Protect a Loved One

You're worried about a loved one's safety. Maybe a younger sibling has just gotten a driver's license or your best friend is heading off to college in a faraway city. This magick potion protects them when you're not around.

WHAT YOU NEED

* A clear glass bottle with a lid or stopper
* A small clear quartz crystal
* Mild soap
* Water (to wash the bottle and crystal)
* Black paint
* Water (to make tea)
* Comfrey tea bags (available from many supermarkets, health food stores, or online)

BEST TIME TO PERFORM THE SPELL
During the new moon

WHAT TO DO

1. Cast a circle around your kitchen. Wash the bottle and the crystal with mild soap and water, then let them dry. Paint a pentagram on the side of the bottle.

2. Heat the water and add the comfrey tea bags. Allow it to steep for several minutes, then cool. Pour the tea into the bottle. Add the quartz crystal. Put the lid or stopper on the bottle and shake it three times to charge it. Open the circle. Let the potion sit overnight, preferably where the moon can shine on it.

3. Remove the crystal and give the protection potion to your loved one. If you're afraid this person will think you're weird, you can transfer the tea into another container *sans* pentagram—the tea will retain the imprint of the symbol. Instruct him or her to drink a little each day.

Charm for Your Guardian Angel

According to many spiritual traditions, everyone has a personal guardian angel who is always there to provide guidance and protection. This magick charm reminds you that your angelic helper is near at hand whenever a challenging situation seems bigger than you can handle.

WHAT YOU NEED

* A small silver or gold hanging charm in the shape of an angel
* A white cord or ribbon 18 inches long
* Amber essential oil

BEST TIME TO PERFORM THE SPELL

On a Saturday

WHAT TO DO

1. Cast a circle around the area where you will do your spell. Slide the charm on the cord or ribbon and tie a knot to make a pendant necklace. As you tie the knot, envision yourself safe, happy, and healthy. Say the following incantation aloud:

   "Guardian angel, be with me.
   Keep me healthy, safe, and free.
   Guide my steps so I may see
   What I must do. Blessed be."

2. Put a dot of amber essential oil on the angel charm. Inhale the scent and let it calm your nerves. You may sense your guardian angel nearby. Envision yourself placing your concerns in the angel's hands, knowing that everything will be taken care of. Slip the necklace over your head and wear it for protection. Open the circle.

Ritual ℞ Call for Angelic Assistance

With this ritual you ask for help and protection by calling upon the archangels: Raphael, Michael, Gabriel, and Uriel. Perform this ritual alone to petition their aid or do it in conjunction with other spells.

WHAT YOU NEED

- ★ 1 yellow votive candle
- ★ 1 red votive candle
- ★ 1 blue votive candle
- ★ 1 green votive candle
- ★ Matches or a lighter

BEST TIME TO PERFORM THE SPELL

Any time

WHAT TO DO

1. Stand facing east and set the yellow candle on the ground (or floor) in front of you, where it can burn safely. Light the candle and say aloud: "Archangel Raphael, Guardian of the East, come and be with me in this sacred space. I request your protection and guidance in all I do, now and always."

2. Move clockwise until you are facing south, and set the red candle on the ground (or floor) in front of you. Light the candle and say aloud: "Archangel Michael, Guardian of the South, come and be with me in this sacred space. I request your protection and guidance in all I do, now and always."

3. Move clockwise until you are facing west, and set the blue candle on the ground (or floor) in front of you. Light the candle and say aloud: "Archangel Gabriel, Guardian of the West, come and be with me in this sacred space. I request your protection and guidance in all I do, now and always."

4. Move clockwise until you are facing north, and set the green candle on the ground (or floor) in front of you. Light the candle and say aloud: "Archangel Uriel, Guardian of the North, come and be with me in this sacred space. I request your protection and guidance in all I do, now and always."

5. Stand in the center of the circle you've cast. Close your eyes and envision the four archangels standing around you, like sentries protecting you from harm. Feel their power flowing into you, filling you with strength and confidence. Remain in the center of the circle for as long as you wish. If you like, you can perform another spell or ritual now, under the watchful guard of the archangels. When you are ready, open the circle in the following manner.

6. Go to the east and stand facing outward. Say aloud: "Archangel Raphael, Guardian of the East, I thank you for your presence here this night (or day). Please continue to guide and protect me always and all ways, even after you return to your home in the heavens. Hail, farewell, and blessed be." Extinguish the yellow candle.

7. Move counterclockwise to the north and stand facing outward. Say aloud: "Archangel Uriel, Guardian of the North, I thank you for your presence here this night (or day). Please continue to guide and protect me always and all ways, even after you return to your home in the heavens. Hail, farewell, and blessed be." Extinguish the green candle.

8. Go to the west and stand facing outward. Say aloud: "Archangel Gabriel, Guardian of the West, I thank you for your presence here this night (or day). Please continue to guide and protect me always and all ways, even after you return to your home in the heavens. Hail, farewell, and blessed be." Extinguish the blue candle.

9. Go to the south and stand facing outward. Say aloud: "Archangel Michael, Guardian of the South, I thank you for your presence here this night (or day). Please continue to guide and protect me always and all ways, even after you return to your home in the heavens. Hail, farewell, and blessed be." Extinguish the red candle.

Amulet to Protect Your Pet

Worried that your beloved pet might wander into harm's way? Can magick really protect Fluffy or Fido? Of course! You can create an amulet for your animal companion just as you would for a human being. Here's how.

WHAT YOU NEED

* ★ Scissors
* ★ Jeweler's elastic
* ★ Tiny amber beads with holes through them

BEST TIME TO PERFORM THE SPELL

Any time

WHAT TO DO

1. Cast a circle around the area where you will do your spell. Cut a piece of stretchy jeweler's elastic long enough to fit over your pet's head. It shouldn't be so loose that your pet can slip out of it easily, nor so tight that it's uncomfortable around their neck. Leave enough elastic to tie a knot when you're finished.

2. String the beads on the elastic, one at a time. With each bead say the following affirmation aloud: "[Pet's name] is safe and sound at all times and in all situations, now and always." Visualize a ball of white light surrounding your pet, keeping them safe. When you've finished, tie a knot and repeat the affirmation a final time. Open the circle. Slip the protection collar over your pet's head.

Wreath 🗘 Protect from Holiday Stress

Holidays can be stressful times, even under the best of circumstances. This special table wreath does double duty— it serves as a great decoration while emitting good vibes to protect your sanity during the hectic holiday season.

WHAT YOU NEED

- A piece of cardboard or poster board
- Scissors
- Lots of dried bay leaves
- Tacky glue, double-sided tape, or other fixative
- 1 white pillar candle in a glass holder

BEST TIME TO PERFORM THE SPELL

As needed

WHAT TO DO

1. Cast a circle around the area where you will do your spell. Cut a circle from the cardboard or poster board, then cut a hole in the center to make a "donut" large enough to slip over the candle in its holder. Attach the bay leaves onto the cardboard circle to make a wreath. Think peaceful thoughts as you work.

2. When you've finished, open the magick circle and set the candle on your table, altar, or mantel. Slide the bay leaf wreath over it, so it circles the base of the candle.

Spell to Distract Nosy Neighbors

Your neighbors are nosy. Remind them to mind their own business with this spell that's sure to stop them from making unwanted visits or comments.

WHAT YOU NEED

★ **A table knife**　　　★ **A mirror**

BEST TIME TO PERFORM THE SPELL

On a Saturday or during the new moon

WHAT TO DO

1. Stand in the center of your home. Hold the knife and point it at your neighbors' home. Keeping your arm outstretched and the knife pointing outward, walk in a clockwise direction around the room/area until you've completed drawing a circle with the knife. Envision a protective wall encircling your home, blocking your neighbors' view. Lay the knife on the windowsill that faces or is closest to your neighbors' home. Say this incantation aloud:
   "I'm protected by this knife
   [Neighbors' name] get a life."

2. Hang the mirror so it faces your neighbors' home. If possible, hang it outside so it reflects their home. If that's not possible, position it at the window where you've laid the knife, so that the mirror faces your neighbors' home. The mirror symbolically deflects their curiosity and bounces their own energy back to them.

3. Say this incantation aloud:
"You'll no longer bother me
What I do you cannot see."

4. Leave the mirror and knife in place until your neighbors find something else to occupy their time and leave you alone.

Amulet ᴛᴏʀ Safe Travels

Are you about to embark on a road trip? Need help battling road rage? This amulet provides extra car protection wherever you go. It also helps prevent breakdowns and wards off car thieves. And if you do experience problems on the road, it works to bring the assistance you need.

WHAT YOU NEED

* **Three amber beads with holes**
* **Three bloodstone beads with holes**
* **Three turquoise beads with holes**
* **Mild soap**
* **Water**
* **A soft cloth**
* **Frankincense incense**
* **An incense burner**
* **Matches or a lighter**
* **A small silver pentagram**
* **Jeweler's wire**

BEST TIME TO PERFORM THE SPELL

On a Saturday, preferably when the sun and/or moon is in Gemini or Sagittarius

WHAT TO DO

1. Wash the gemstones with mild soap and water, then pat them dry with the soft cloth. Cast a circle around the area where you will do your spell. Fit the incense in its burner and light it. Attach one end of the jeweler's wire to the pentagram. Then string the beads on the wire one at a time, alternating them. Leave enough wire to hang the gemstone amulet from the rearview mirror of your car. As you work, envision yourself in your car with a bubble of white light surrounding you.

2. When you've finished stringing the beads, hold the amulet in the incense smoke for a few moments to charge it. Repeat this incantation aloud three times:
   "Wherever I go, the world around
   This amulet keeps me safe and sound."

3. Open the circle and hang the gemstone amulet from your car's rearview mirror.

Spell to Protect from Bad Vibes

Locks on your doors and windows will deter human threats, but what about psychic ones? If you fear that someone is sending you "bad vibes" try this herbal protection spell.

WHAT YOU NEED

* A large pot
* 2 quarts of water
* A bunch of fresh basil
* A strainer
* A pitcher

BEST TIME TO PERFORM THE SPELL

On a Saturday, preferably when the sun and/or moon is in Capricorn

WHAT TO DO

1. Heat the water in the pot. Add the basil and let it simmer for ten minutes. Allow the brew to cool. Strain the basil out and pour the water into a pitcher. Set the basil aside to dry; save it to use in other spells.

2. Take the pitcher of basil-infused water outside and pour it on the ground near your front door, drawing a pentagram with the liquid. Repeat the process at your back door (and any other doors that lead into your home). As you mark the ground with the pentagrams, say this incantation aloud:

   "My home is now protected at all times,
   In all situations,
   Always and all ways."

Pillow FOR Nighttime Protection

Are racing thoughts and bad dreams keeping you from getting a good night's sleep? This fragrant protection pillow calms your nerves and helps you relax, so you can stop worrying and get a good night's sleep.

WHAT YOU NEED

- ★ Two squares of dark blue cloth, 3 inches × 3 inches or larger
- ★ White thread
- ★ A needle
- ★ Dried basil leaves
- ★ Fennel seeds
- ★ Rosemary
- ★ Dried parsley
- ★ Dried ash leaves
- ★ Lavender flowers
- ★ Lemongrass
- ★ Sage

BEST TIME TO PERFORM THE SPELL
During the new moon

WHAT TO DO

1. Cast a circle around the area where you will do your spell. Using the white thread and needle, sew the squares of blue cloth together on three sides—it's best if you do it by hand, rather than with a sewing machine. When you've finished, fill the casing with the herbs. Sew the fourth side closed to make a tiny pillow.

2. Open the circle. Lay the protection pillow beside your regular bed pillow so you can smell its soothing scent during the night.

Spell ᖴᗝᖇ Help from Your Spirit Animal

According to shamanic traditions, spirit animal guardians provide protection and guidance in this world and beyond. Do you feel an affinity with a particular animal? That could be your spirit animal guide or totem.

WHAT YOU NEED

* 1 black candle
* 1 white candle
* 2 candleholders
* Matches or a lighter
* A photo, figurine, painting, or other image of the animal whose help you are soliciting

BEST TIME TO PERFORM THE SPELL

Any time

WHAT TO DO

1. Cast a circle around the area where you will do your spell. Fit the candles in their holders and set them on your altar (or another surface, such as a tabletop). As you face the altar, the black candle should be at your left and the white one on your right. Light the candles and place the image of the animal between them.

2. Gaze at the animal image. Sense this animal's presence near you, not necessarily as a physical creature but as a spirit being who will accompany you wherever and whenever you need them. Breathe slowly and deeply, bringing into yourself the qualities you seek from that animal: strength, courage, speed, cunning, and so on. Feel your fear ebbing away. Ask this animal to share any suggestions that might help you. An answer may come in the form of a vision, insight, sensation, sound, scent, or inner knowing.

3. When you feel ready, extinguish the candles and pick up the image of your animal guardian. Open the circle. Carry the image with you for protection and reassurance.

Garden to Protect Your Home

Not only will gardening make your yard look nice, it can also be a powerful way to protect your home. Choose some plants from the list below, depending on where you live and which plants you like best. If you're not ready for a whole garden, try growing some plants in window boxes or flowerpots. Warning: some favorite plants of protection are poisonous, so if you decide to include them in your garden, make sure they won't be accessible to children or pets. Also, wear gardening gloves while working with these plants.

WHAT YOU NEED

* A gardening trowel or shovel
* Gardening gloves
* As many of the following plants as you wish to include in your garden: white snapdragons, basil, white peonies, St. John's wort, foxglove (poisonous), aconite (poisonous), garlic, fennel, white clover, thyme, ferns, poppies (poisonous), rosemary, yucca, cactus, blessed thistle

BEST TIME TO PERFORM THE SPELL

During the waxing moon, preferably when the moon is in Taurus

WHAT TO DO

Plant the flowers and herbs you've chosen, according to their particular soil and light requirements. As you work, envision them providing a protective shield around your residence. Ask the plants to safeguard you and your home. Care for the plants and they'll continue to care for you.

Amulet to Protect Your Finances

Are rising expenses, a lost job, or even increasing debts threatening your financial security? This amulet helps to protect your assets and give you some peace of mind about your money.

WHAT YOU NEED

- A piece of aventurine
- A piece of onyx
- Mild soap
- Water
- A soft cloth
- A black marker
- A circular piece of soft, flexible leather
- (deerskin is perfect), 8 inches in diameter
- A single-hole paper punch
- A leather thong
- Alfalfa
- A cauldron
- Matches or a lighter

BEST TIME TO PERFORM THE SPELL

On a Saturday

WHAT TO DO

1. Wash the gemstones with mild soap and water, then pat them dry with the soft cloth. Cast a circle around the area where you will do your spell. It should be a place where you can burn a small fire safely. With the marker, draw a pentagram on the inside center of the leather circle. With the paper punch, make small holes around the outside of the leather circle, large enough that you can slide the thong through them. Thread the thong through the holes. Pull up the outer edges of the circle, tightening the thong to form a pouch (with the pentagram inside on the bottom).

2. Put the alfalfa in the cauldron. Light it and let it burn completely. Allow the ashes to cool. Pour the ashes into the pouch, then add the gemstones. Close the pouch and tie three knots in the thong. Open the circle.

3. Place the amulet in the wealth sector of your home or business. To locate this, stand at the entrance to your home (the one you use most often, not necessarily the front door) with your back to the door so you're looking inside. The rear left-hand corner is the wealth sector. If you prefer, put the amulet in your safe, cash register, or purse to safeguard your finances.

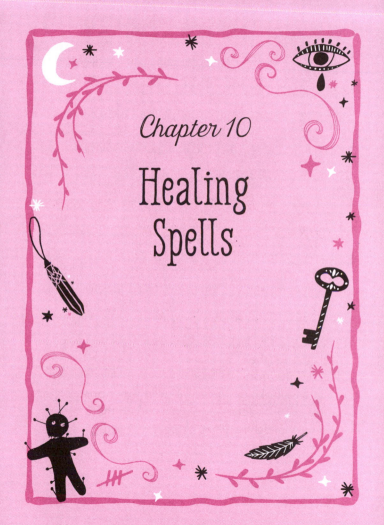

Chapter 10

Healing Spells

Your racing mind is keeping you awake at all hours of the night. Your best friend has come down with a cold that just won't seem to quit. Your partner overdid it at the gym and you can't stand listening to them complain about their sore muscles another second longer. Time to whip up some magick to cure whatever ails you! Remember: magick spells are not a substitute for professional care. It's also important to remember that sometimes an illness has a purpose and can point us toward other parts of our lives that need a change. For instance, if you find yourself fighting the flu, that might be a sign that you've been working too hard and need a rest. The same goes for other people. Although it seems compassionate to want to help others, always ask, either directly or by speaking to that person's higher self, if it's really the right thing to do for their overall well-being.

Spell ⟶ Soothe the Common Cold

It's cold and flu season, and you're definitely not at your best. A little herbal magick plus some TLC can relieve those miserable symptoms fast and make you feel better all over.

WHAT YOU NEED

- Spring water
- Hyssop leaves and flowers
- A strainer
- A bathtub
- 1 aqua beeswax candle with a cotton wick
- 1 candleholder
- Matches or a lighter

BEST TIME TO PERFORM THE SPELL
As needed

WHAT TO DO

1. Brew a strong tea from the spring water and hyssop leaves and/or flowers. Strain the herb residue from the water. Fill a bathtub with comfortably hot water and add the tea to it. Fit the candle in its holder and light it. Get into the tub and soak for as long as you like, inhaling the soothing scent of hyssop.

2. Focus your mind on loving thoughts and feelings. Envision yourself surrounded by love. As you inhale, imagine you are bringing love into your body. See and sense love circulating throughout your entire body, from head to foot. Spend several minutes doing this. Let the loving energy gently nourish you, strengthening your system so it can throw off the cold.

3. Remain in the tub for as long as you like. After you get out of the bathwater, extinguish the candle. Repeat this ritual whenever you like.

Potion FOR Healthy Weight Loss

Your jeans are getting tight and you're not sure you want to be seen in a swimsuit just now. Other than the usual diet and exercise regime, is there anything you can do to safely shed those unwanted pounds? This magick potion works at a subconscious level to silence hunger pangs and prevent overeating.

WHAT YOU NEED

- ★ Spring water
- ★ Unsweetened green apple tea (not spiced apple)
- ★ A hot pink ceramic cup
- ★ 1 hot pink candle
- ★ 1 candleholder
- ★ Matches or a lighter

BEST TIME TO PERFORM THE SPELL

During the waning moon

WHAT TO DO

1. When you feel hungry, instead of eating something you shouldn't, brew a pot of green apple tea using spring water. Pour the tea into the bright pink cup. Fit the candle into its holder, set it on the dining room or kitchen table, and light it. Sit and gaze at the candle while you inhale the refreshing scent of the tea.

2. Drink the cup of tea slowly, keeping your attention focused on the candle. Feel your hunger pangs gradually subside. Repeat as necessary.

Spell for a Speedy Recovery

An illness or injury has you temporarily sidelined. This simple spell uses the color green, symbolizing healthy plants, to aid your recovery. Repeat it often and you'll be back in the game soon.

WHAT YOU NEED

* A green ribbon long enough to tie around the afflicted body part
* A green light bulb or green filter that will color the light from an ordinary lamp

BEST TIME TO PERFORM THE SPELL

During the waxing moon to promote new tissue growth or to increase vitality; during the waning moon to eliminate an unwanted condition or to decrease unpleasant symptoms

WHAT TO DO

1. Tie the ribbon comfortably around the part of your body that is injured or ailing. Make sure it doesn't interfere with an open wound or other skin damage. As you tie it, say aloud: "I am radiantly healthy and whole, in body, mind, and spirit."

2. Shine the green light on the afflicted area for a few minutes, while you visualize yourself completely healed. Don't think about the injury or illness; imagine the end result you desire instead.

3. Repeat this "green light" treatment several times a day. Leave the ribbon in place until the condition is healed, then remove it and burn it.

Spell ᶠᴼᴿ Healing Energy

This spell draws upon the powers of heaven and Earth to help heal any condition. What's great about this spell is that you can do it for yourself or for someone else, even if the other person isn't physically present. Just remember to ask that person's permission first.

WHAT YOU NEED
★ **A magick wand**

BEST TIME TO PERFORM THE SPELL
Any time

WHAT TO DO
1. Cast a circle around yourself. If you are doing the spell for another person who is physically present, cast the circle around both of you. Stand in the center of the circle with your feet about shoulder-width apart.

2. Close your eyes. Hold the wand over your head with both hands, with your arms outstretched and straight. Point the tip of the wand at the sky and say aloud: "With this wand I draw down the healing force of the heavens." In your mind's eye see light flowing into the wand, making it glow brightly.

3. Open your eyes and point the tip of the wand at the afflicted part of your body (or the other person's). If the person for whom you are doing this spell is not physically present, aim the wand toward his or her location. Envision the light you collected from the heavens flowing into the injured or ailing body part, zapping it with healing rays.

4. When you sense that all the light has been transferred from the wand to the body, point the wand at the ground. Close your eyes and say aloud: "With this wand I draw up the healing force of Mother Earth." In your mind's eye see light flowing into the wand from the center of the Earth, making it glow brightly.

5. Open your eyes and aim the tip of the wand at the afflicted part of your body (or the other person's). Envision the light you collected from the earth flowing into the injured or ailing body part, zapping it with healing rays until all the light has been transferred from the wand to the body. When you've finished, thank the forces of heaven and Earth for assisting you and open the circle.

Spell € Cure a Headache

It's been a stressful day and your head feels like someone is tightening a clamp around it. The key to this spell is detaching yourself from the pain, rather than resisting it.

WHAT YOU NEED

★ **Nothing but yourself**

BEST TIME TO PERFORM THE SPELL

Any time

WHAT TO DO

1. Sit in a comfortable place. Close your eyes. Acknowledge the presence of the pain, rather than fighting it. Don't identify with it, however. Envision it as something that's not a part of you. Mentally step back, so that your awareness is slightly above and outside your head, and simply observe the pain without emotion.

2. Hold your thumb and your index finger on either side of the back of your neck, where it joins the base of the skull. Apply firm pressure for a minute or more, while you breathe slowly and deeply. Each time you inhale, imagine taking clear light blue air into your lungs. See the soothing blue air rise into your head and gently swirl around inside your skull.

3. After a minute or so, let go of your neck and press your index finger to your "third eye," in the middle of your forehead.

4. Continue breathing in blue air for a minute or two. Release the pressure on your third eye and hold your index fingers to your temples. Apply firm pressure for at least a minute, while you inhale healing blue light, then release. Open your eyes. Repeat as necessary.

Ritual ᖴᴏʀ Less Stress

While you may not be able to avoid stress all the time, you can definitely keep it from getting you down. This ritual helps you release stress and stay calm in the presence of everyday annoyances.

WHAT YOU NEED

- A tumbled chunk of amethyst
- A tumbled chunk of rose quartz
- Mild soap
- Water
- A soft cloth
- Soothing music (New Age or classical is best, either instrumental or chanting, without a catchy rhythm or lyrics)
- A ballpoint pen
- Lavender, vanilla, sweet orange, or ylang-ylang essential oil
- 1 blue candle
- 1 candleholder
- Matches or a lighter

BEST TIME TO PERFORM THE SPELL

Any time

WHAT TO DO

1. Wash the gemstones with mild soap and water, then pat them dry with the soft cloth. Start the music you've chosen. Cast a circle around the area where you will do your spell. With the ballpoint pen inscribe the word *peace* on the candle. Dress the candle by rubbing a little essential oil on it (not on the wick). Fit the candle in its holder and light it.

2. Hold one gemstone in each hand. Sit in a comfortable place and close your eyes. Begin breathing slowly and deeply. Inhale the soothing scent and allow it to calm your mind. Rub the smooth stones with your fingers. Feel the stones neutralize stress, irritability, and anxiety. Focus on your breathing, paying attention to each inhalation and exhalation. If your mind starts to wander, gently bring it back and say or think the word *peace*.

3. Spend at least ten minutes this way, longer if you wish. When you feel ready, open your eyes and extinguish the candle. Open the circle. Let the music continue playing or shut it off. Carry the stones with you and rub them whenever stress starts to mount.

Spell FOR Sweet Dreams Only

You need your sleep, but when you do doze off, bad dreams disturb your rest. This bedtime ritual relaxes your mind so you can get a good night's sleep. Do this spell at least fifteen minutes after brushing your teeth, as mint toothpaste or mouthwash will nullify the effects of the white chestnut.

WHAT YOU NEED

★ A piece of amethyst
★ Mild soap
★ Water
★ A soft cloth
★ 1 dark blue votive candle
★ Matches or a lighter
★ A glass of spring water
★ 4 drops white chestnut flower essence (available from health food stores or online)
★ A piece of paper
★ A pen or pencil

BEST TIME TO PERFORM THE SPELL

Before going to bed

WHAT TO DO

1. Wash the amethyst with mild soap and water, and pat it dry with the soft cloth. Light the votive candle and spend a few moments gazing into the flame to relax your mind. Put four drops of white chestnut flower essence in the glass of water and sip it slowly. On the paper, make a list of all the things you must remember to do tomorrow. Once you've written down these tasks your mind can stop reminding you of them.

2. Turn the paper over and draw the *I Ching* hexagram *T'ai/Peace* on it. This symbol consists of six lines stacked one on top of the other. Each of the top three lines looks like two dashes side by side. The bottom three lines are solid. Lay the piece of paper on your nightstand with the *I Ching* hexagram facing up. Set the amethyst on top of the symbol.

3. Extinguish the candle. Get into bed and feel the soothing resonances of the flower essence and the amethyst quieting your thoughts. If your mind strays to worrisome matters, gently stop yourself and replace those thoughts with a mental image of the symbol *T'ai*.

Potion ᶠᴼᴿ a Good Night's Sleep

This magick potion will quiet your thoughts and emotions so you can sleep better. It can also inspire prophetic dreams as well as dreams that offer guidance in your waking hours.

WHAT YOU NEED

- ★ A silver or silver-plated bowl
- ★ A moonstone
- ★ Mild soap
- ★ Water
- ★ Spring water
- ★ A glass bottle with a cap or stopper

BEST TIME TO PERFORM THE SPELL

During the full moon

WHAT TO DO

1. On the night of the full moon, wash the bowl and the moonstone with mild soap and water, then place the stone in the bowl. Fill the bowl with spring water. Set it where the moon will be reflected in the water. Allow the water to sit overnight. In the morning, remove the moonstone and pour the moon-imprinted water into the bottle.

2. Each night before retiring, sip a little of the potion to help you sleep better. Pay attention to your dreams too—they may hold answers to daily dilemmas or offer glimpses into the future. Make a new batch of this potion at each full moon.

Potion To Keep Your Cool

This magick potion helps you beat the heat, whether it's physical or psychological. The secret ingredient is aquamarine, a pale blue gem whose name comes from the Latin word for seawater. This potion is meant for drinking, or you could also soak a clean cotton cloth in the potion to make a cooling poultice. Lay the cloth on your forehead to ease a headache or over your eyes to soothe eyestrain.

WHAT YOU NEED

* An aquamarine
* Mild soap
* Water
* A chalice
* Spring water

BEST TIME TO PERFORM THE SPELL
Any time

WHAT TO DO
1. Wash the aquamarine with mild soap and water. Cast a circle around the area where you will do your spell. Place the aquamarine in the bottom of your chalice, then fill the chalice with water.

2. Swirl the water in the chalice in a counterclockwise direction to charge it, while you chant this incantation:
"I am healed
In body and mind
Of imbalances
Of any kind."

3. Remove the aquamarine. As you drink the potion, imagine you are immersing yourself in a refreshing pool of water to keep your cool. Open the circle. Store unused water in the fridge, preferably in a clear glass bottle, and keep some on hand for emergencies.

Herb Garden for Healing

Early healers grew their own medicinal and magick herbs to cure all manner of illness. You, too, can grow a magick herb garden and have fresh, healing herbs available when you need them for teas, poultices, lotions, balms, and spells. If you don't have space for an outdoor garden, plant herbs in flowerpots or window boxes. Start with a few and add to your garden as your skills and needs expand.

WHAT YOU NEED

* Aloe (for burns, constipation, and stomach ulcers)
* Basil (for insect stings and bites)
* Blackberry (for diarrhea, colds, and sore throats)
* Chamomile (for digestive disorders, nervous conditions, and insomnia)
* Comfrey (for congestion and stomach complaints)
* Dandelion (for skin disorders)
* Echinacea (for colds and flu)
* Garlic (to clean wounds and prevent infection)
* Lavender (for relaxation)
* Marigold (for rashes, eczema, and skin irritations)
* Parsley (to cleanse the kidneys and liver)
* Peppermint (for nausea and colds)
* Raspberry (for female complaints)
* Rosemary (for headaches and insomnia)
* Sage (to staunch bleeding; for sore muscles)
* St. John's wort (for bronchitis and lung congestion)
* Verbena (for coughs, breathing difficulties, and fevers)

BEST TIME TO PLANT

During the waxing moon, preferably when the sun or moon is in Taurus or Virgo

WHAT TO DO

1. Consider every step of your gardening process—planting, watering, tending, and harvesting—to be a magickal act. Invite the nature spirits to assist you.

2. Talk to your plants and thank them for helping you, especially when you harvest them.

Ritual FOR Clear, Radiant Skin

Are you bothered by skin imperfections or annoying spots on your face? When you do this simple ritual you focus positive energy onto your face to clear and rejuvenate your skin.

WHAT YOU NEED

★ **Nothing but yourself**

BEST TIME TO PERFORM THE SPELL

Every day

WHAT TO DO

1. Close your eyes and begin breathing slowly and deeply. Rub your palms together vigorously, until they feel quite warm. Beginning at your collarbones, hold your hands an inch or so away from your body with your palms turned toward you. Move your hands upward, over your face, to the top of your head. When you get to the top of your head, flick your hands sharply as if throwing off water—you are actually shaking off unwanted energy.

2. As you move your hands, imagine you are drawing off all the tension and impurities that lead to pimples, dryness, and other imperfections. Envision healing, invigorating energy infusing your skin with good health. Repeat these movements six more times (for a total of seven passes). Perform this quick and easy ritual each morning and each night to stimulate your own inherent vitality and regenerative abilities.

Lotion FOR Post-Gym Aches

You've overdone it at the gym and now your muscles are making their displeasure known. This herbal balm helps soothe sore muscles and relieve minor aches and pains.

WHAT YOU NEED

- A glass jar, bottle, or other container with a lid
- A small clear quartz crystal
- Mild soap
- Water
- A soft cloth
- 9 ounces of olive, almond, or grape seed oil
- 2 drops camphor essential oil
- 2 drops clove essential oil
- 2 drops lavender essential oil
- Fresh ginger
- A grater

BEST TIME TO PERFORM THE SPELL
As needed

WHAT TO DO

1. Wash the jar/bottle and the crystal with mild soap and water, then pat them dry with a soft cloth. Cast a circle around the area where you will do your spell. Pour the olive, almond, or grape seed oil into the bottle. Add two drops of each essential oil. Grate the fresh ginger very fine and add a little to the oil mixture.

2. Hold the quartz crystal to your "third eye," in the middle of your forehead, and send a vision of soothing, healing energy into the crystal. You might see it as blue or green light. Then put the crystal into the oil mixture and cap the jar/bottle. Shake the jar/bottle three times to charge it. Open the circle. Rub the healing lotion on your sore muscles to alleviate pain. Repeat as necessary.

Spell to Soothe Sore Eyes

You didn't get enough sleep last night, and all day you've been staring at a computer screen. Now your poor eyes feel like they're full of sand. Instead of using over-the-counter eye drops, try this quick spell to ease soreness and fatigue.

WHAT YOU NEED

★ **Nothing but yourself**

BEST TIME TO PERFORM THE SPELL
Any time

WHAT TO DO
Rub your hands together vigorously for a few moments, until your palms are very warm. Close your eyes and relax. Hold your palms over your eyes, letting the stimulating energy you've raised provide comfort and rejuvenation. Repeat as necessary.

Dance FOR Health and Happiness

Dancing has long been used as a form of therapy for all types of ailments. It is taught at hospitals and mental health facilities as a fun way to treat emotional as well as physical ills. It works like magick to chase your blues away and it's great exercise! Ask a friend or partner to join you for added fun.

WHAT YOU NEED
★ **Lively music (salsa, country, rock 'n' roll, disco— whatever makes you start tapping your feet)**

BEST TIME TO PERFORM THE SPELL
Any time

WHAT TO DO
1. Play the music and start moving your body to the beat. Don't worry what you look like or if you're doing it right. Start slow if you're out of shape. Try to stay loose and fluid.

2. Change rhythm from time to time, and notice how different movements make you feel. As emotions come up, note them but don't dwell on them.

3. Dance until your breathing quickens, your heart beats faster, and your temperature rises—as long as it's comfortable for you. Just ten minutes a day can make a huge difference in your physical and psychological condition.

Ritual ᴛᴏʀ Reclaiming Energy

Do you feel worn out at the end of the day, especially if you have to deal with a lot of people? According to ancient Toltec teachings, you leave a bit of your own vitality behind with every individual you meet during the day. This ritual lets you reclaim the energy you've given away so you don't get depleted.

WHAT YOU NEED
★ Nothing but yourself

BEST TIME TO PERFORM THE SPELL
At the end of each day, before going to sleep

WHAT TO DO
1. Choose a time when you won't be disturbed; turn off the TV, silence your phone, and so on. Sit in a comfortable chair and close your eyes.

2. Start breathing slowly and deeply. Begin recalling all the people you encountered and all the incidents that occurred during the day, one at a time.

3. Turn your head to the left and remember something that happened in which you participated in some way. Inhale as you revisit the thoughts and feelings you had, as well as the events that took place. Then turn your head to the right and exhale, releasing the experience with your breath. Continue doing this until you've recapped every event of the day, from beginning to end, the little things as well as the big ones. Feel yourself relaxing and gaining strength with each memory you cast out.

4. Repeat this process every night. Daily practice keeps you from draining your natural energy resources.

Ritual to Restore and Re-Energize

It's important to take time for yourself to recharge at the end of a long day. This ritual helps you recover some of the energy you've let other people take from you during the day. Perform it in conjunction with the Ritual for Reclaiming Energy (see previous ritual) or by itself.

WHAT YOU NEED
★ Nothing but yourself

BEST TIME TO PERFORM THE SPELL
At the end of each day, before going to sleep

WHAT TO DO

1. Choose a time when you won't be disturbed; turn off the TV, silence your phone, and so on. Sit in a comfortable chair and close your eyes. Start breathing slowly and deeply. Bring to mind someone you encountered during the day. Imagine that person standing in front of you. Notice any splotches of color that appear to be stuck on that person's body—they represent pieces of your own vital energy that you gave away to someone else.

2. Pick one splotch and as you inhale, imagine you are pulling that colored energy patch off the person's body and drawing it toward yourself. As you exhale, feel the energy being reabsorbed into your body.

3. Continue in this manner until you've taken back all the energy you squandered during the day and reincorporated it into yourself. You'll know you're done when you don't see any more colored spots remaining on that individual's body. Do this for everyone with whom you interacted, so they don't keep draining your vitality.

Ritual FOR Restoring Balance

You're not actually ill, just feeling a bit "blah." Perhaps daily stress and worries have thrown you off-balance. With this magick visualization technique you focus on your body's energy centers, known as chakras, to restore harmony to your entire system.

191

WHAT YOU NEED

★ **Nothing but yourself**

BEST TIME TO PERFORM THE SPELL

Any time

WHAT TO DO

1. Sit in a comfortable chair and close your eyes. Start breathing slowly and deeply. Focus your attention on the base of your spine, the energy center known as the root chakra. Imagine a ball of clear red light glowing there, and feel its warmth radiating in this part of your body for a few moments.

2. Next, focus on the sacral chakra about a hand's width below your belly button. Envision a sphere of orange light shining there. After a few moments shift your attention to your solar plexus; see yellow light radiating and warming this part of your body.

3. Continue breathing rhythmically as you visualize bright green light glowing around your heart. Feel it calming and refreshing you.

4. Move your attention up to the base of your throat and imagine blue light shining there for a few moments.

5. Shift your focus to your third eye, in the middle of your forehead, while you envision indigo light at this point.

6. Finally, allow your attention to go to the crown chakra at the top of your head. As you see purple light resonating there, sense your connection with a higher force. Feel power flowing from the heavens into the top of your head and down your spine, energizing your entire body.

7. Enjoy this pleasant, soothing sensation for as long as you wish. Repeat this revitalizing ritual whenever you feel off-center, stressed out, or tired.

Spell to Balance Your Chakras

Like the Ritual for Restoring Balance (see previous spell), this spell balances the chakras that run from the base of your spine to the top of your head. In this case, however, you utilize the power of gemstones to create harmony and restore your vitality.

WHAT YOU NEED

* A piece of red jasper
* A piece of carnelian
* A piece of topaz
* A piece of jade
* A piece of aquamarine
* A piece of lapis lazuli
* A piece of amethyst
* Mild soap
* Water
* A soft cloth

BEST TIME TO PERFORM THE SPELL
Any time

WHAT TO DO

1. Wash the stones with mild soap and water, then pat them dry with the soft cloth. Cast a circle around the area where you will do your spell, which should be a comfortable place where you can lie down undisturbed for about a half hour. Place the stones where you can reach them easily and lie down on your back.

2. Put the red jasper on your pubic bone. Set the carnelian on your lower abdomen, about a hand's width below your belly button. Position the topaz on your solar plexus. Put the jade on the center of your chest near your heart. Lay the aquamarine at the base of your throat. Rest the lapis lazuli on your forehead, between your eyebrows. Place the amethyst so it touches the crown of your head.

3. Close your eyes. Remain in this position for about half an hour. Relax and sense the stones sending their healing vibrations into your body's energy centers, restoring harmony and well-being to your entire system. When you feel ready, remove the stones and get up. Open the circle. Repeat this ritual whenever you wish.

Potion FOR a Healing Pick-Me-Up

You're feeling under the weather and could use a little magick to soothe what ails you. When you drink this healing brew, you nourish your body, mind, and spirit with herbal medicine and loving energy.

WHAT YOU NEED

* 1 mint herbal tea bag
* A chalice
* An echinacea capsule (available in health food stores and some supermarkets)
* ¼ teaspoon lemon juice
* ½ teaspoon honey
* A silver or silver-plated spoon

BEST TIME TO PERFORM THE SPELL
Any time

WHAT TO DO

1. Brew the mint tea and pour some into your chalice. Open the echinacea capsule and sprinkle the herb into the tea. Add the lemon juice and honey. Stir the tea in the chalice three times, in a clockwise direction, to charge it.

2. Gaze at the chalice and imagine a ray of pink light flowing into the chalice, infusing the tea with healing energy. Then slowly sip the tea. Feel its loving vibrations being absorbed into your body.

3. Feel a tingling warmth radiating in your heart chakra. Allow the healing herbal blend to ease your discomfort and restore your sense of well-being. Repeat as necessary.

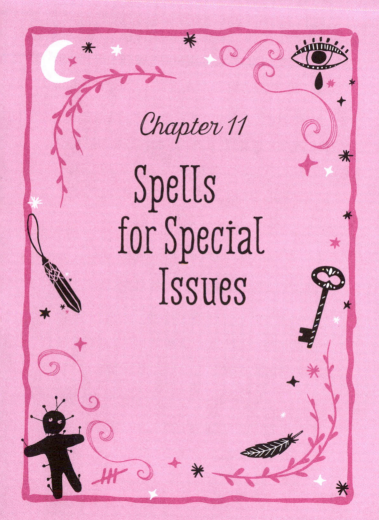

Chapter 11

Spells for Special Issues

You can pretty much count on it—whatever your problem, there's a spell to fix it. And if you can't seem to find one, no need to worry! By now, you have enough spellcasting skills that you may be ready to start designing or adapting spells to suit your specific needs. Check out Chapter 4 for help deciding which colors, herbs, and gemstones will help you most. The spells in this chapter will help you solve a mix of problems, from giving you the courage to overcome a daunting challenge to helping you get in the shortest shopping line at the grocery store. This is the perfect place to start experimenting with what works best for you, since most of these spells use tools and techniques that can be applied to just about anything and can be easily adapted by simply changing a few ingredients. Keep note of the changes you make and get ready to take on the world, one spell at a time!

Spell ⟨FOR⟩ a "Piece of Cake"

A project is taking longer than expected; a romance has hit a snag; you have to deal with a lot of uncooperative people at work or at home. This spell uses "kitchen witchery" to sweeten a frustrating situation. Choose a flavor that suits your intentions: chocolate or strawberry for love; cinnamon or mint for money; almond or vanilla for peace of mind. You don't have to be a gourmet baker to carry off this spell—your intention is what counts.

WHAT YOU NEED

- A cake mix (or ingredients for making your favorite cake recipe)
- Food coloring
- A large bowl
- A large spoon
- Cake pan(s)
- Icing (or ingredients for making your favorite icing recipe)
- Candles
- Matches or a lighter

BEST TIME TO PERFORM THE SPELL

Depends on your intentions (see Chapter 5)

WHAT TO DO

1. Cast a circle around your kitchen. Follow the directions for making the cake, according to the package or your favorite recipe. As you work, focus on your objective and imagine you are sending your intention into the batter.

2. Add food coloring to tint the batter to match your intention: pink for love, green for money, and so on. Using a large spoon, stir the batter in a bowl using a clockwise motion if your goal is to attract something or to stimulate an increase. Stir counterclockwise if you want to limit, decrease, or remove something. Pour the batter into the pan(s) and bake.

3. When the cake has finished cooking, let it cool. Ice it with frosting in a color that relates to your intention. You may want to decorate it with symbols, pictures, and words that also describe your objective.

4. Add candles of an appropriate color. The number of candles should also correspond to your goal: two for love, four for stability, five for change, and so on. Light the candles and concentrate on your wish. Blow out the candles. Share the cake with other people, if you like, or eat it yourself. Each person who partakes incorporates the intention into him- or herself and becomes a cocreator in the spell's success.

Spell to Call for Help

You're confused about how to handle a challenging situation. No matter how hard you rack your brain, you never seem to come to the right answer. Whatever your problem is, there's a deity who can help. This spell invokes divine assistance through burning incense. As the smoke rises, it carries your request into the heavens.

WHAT YOU NEED

* ★ A picture, figurine, or other image of your chosen deity
* ★ Incense
* ★ An incense burner
* ★ Matches or a lighter
* ★ A slip of paper
* ★ A pen or pencil

BEST TIME TO PERFORM THE SPELL

Depends on your intentions (see Chapter 5)

WHAT TO DO

1. Display the image or figurine of your chosen god or goddess on your altar.
2. Select an incense that corresponds to your intentions. Fit the incense into its burner and light it.
3. Write your request on the slip of paper, fold it three times, and lay it at the feet of the deity. Envision your request floating up to the heavens, carried on the incense smoke to your chosen god or goddess.
4. Quiet your mind and listen for an answer or guidance. Allow the incense to burn down completely. Thank the deity for helping you and trust that aid will come at the appropriate time. Remember: the answer might not come immediately (it could take a few days), so don't grow impatient.

Ritual ꝼᴏʀ Fearlessness

Although some fears are admittedly real, many of the things we worry about never happen. Like monsters in a nightmare, if you stand up to unfounded fears they lose their power. In this ritual, you face four of your fears and befriend them.

WHAT YOU NEED

- ★ A bell
- ★ Incense
- ★ An incense burner
- ★ Matches or a lighter
- ★ 1 red votive candle
- ★ A bottle of jasmine essential oil
- ★ A small crystal

BEST TIME TO PERFORM THE SPELL

During the waning moon

WHAT TO DO

1. Cast a circle around the area where you will do your spell. Stand facing east. Ring the bell as you call to mind a fear that involves communication, intellectual matters, or travel. Sense the fear as a presence (but not as an actual person you know). Tell it you aren't going to let it intimidate you anymore. Then say you've come to make peace with it, that you want it to go away, and that you have brought it a gift. Select an incense that corresponds to your intentions. Fit the incense in its burner and light it. Set the incense in a place where it can burn safely. Ring the bell again to dismiss the fear and say: "Accept this gift and be gone."

2. Move clockwise until you're facing south. Ring the bell as you call to mind a fear that involves your public image, creativity, or asserting yourself. Sense the fear as a presence before you (but not as an actual person you know). Tell it you aren't going to let it prevent you from doing what you want and love to do. Then say you've come to make peace with it, that you want it to go away and leave you alone, and that you have brought it a gift. Set the candle in a spot where it can burn safely and light it. Ring the bell again to dismiss the fear and say: "Accept this gift and be gone."

3. Move clockwise until you're facing west. Ring the bell as you call to mind a fear that involves an emotional situation or a relationship with another person. Sense the fear as a presence before you (but not as an actual person you know). Tell it you aren't going to let it make you feel weak and vulnerable. Then say you've come to make peace with it, that you want it to go away and leave you alone, and that you have brought it a gift. Set the bottle of essential oil on the ground or floor. Ring the bell again to dismiss the fear and say: "Accept this gift and be gone."

4. Continue moving clockwise until you're facing north. Ring the bell as you call to mind a fear that involves money, property, or security. Sense the fear as a presence before you (but not as an actual person you know). Tell it you aren't going to let it weigh

you down. Then say you've come to make peace with it, that you want it to go away and leave you alone, and that you have brought it a gift. Set the crystal on the ground or floor. Ring the bell again to dismiss the fear and say: "Accept this gift and be gone."

5. Stand in the center of the circle and imagine your fears growing smaller and smaller. Envision them creeping away; these fears are no longer threats to you. When you feel ready, open the circle. Repeat this ritual as needed, calling up different fears as they arise. Since these gifts are symbolic, they can be removed from the circle and reused.

Charm Bracelet 𝐅𝐎𝐑 Intentions

You may already have a charm bracelet covered with tiny symbols that represent your interests or achievements. The symbols on this charm bracelet, however, represent your desires and intentions. Keeping these symbols in your immediate energy field makes this bracelet work, well, like a charm.

WHAT YOU NEED
★ A silver or gold link bracelet
★ Small charms that can be attached to the bracelet

BEST TIME TO PERFORM THE SPELL
Any time

WHAT TO DO

1. Choose a bracelet that holds as many charms as you have wishes. Wear a metal that harmonizes with your goals. For instance, silver embodies feminine qualities and corresponds to the moon. Its energy is receptive, intuitive, emotional, and works through the power of attraction. Gold signifies masculine qualities and relates to the sun. Its energy is active, direct, logical, and works through the power of assertion.

2. Select charms that hold meaning for you and that depict your objectives. If your goal is to attract a partner, a heart is an apt symbol. A car or airplane might represent travel. It's okay to combine talismans to attract things you desire with amulets to repel things you prefer to keep at bay. Wear as many charms as you like. Add or remove them over time as your intentions change. Remember to wash your charms before wearing them, to get rid of any lingering energies left behind by other people who may have touched them.

Spell for Three Wishes

Like the genie in Aladdin's magick lamp, this spell grants you three wishes to turn bad days into good ones. When choosing the lamp found in this spell, try to find an old-fashioned oil lamp made of brass, tin, copper, or silver; otherwise, substitute an incense burner with a lid that has perforations in it to allow the smoke to float out.

WHAT YOU NEED

* ★ Incense
* ★ A metal oil lamp or a covered incense burner
* ★ Matches or a lighter

BEST TIME TO PERFORM THE SPELL

Depends on your intentions (see Chapter 5)

WHAT TO DO

1. Cast a circle around the area where you will do your spell.
2. Select an incense that corresponds to your intentions. Fit the incense into the lamp or incense burner and light it. Put the lid on so the smoke rises from the spout or perforations. Hold your hands on either side of the lamp/ incense burner (but don't actually touch it if the sides are hot) and pretend to rub it. Envision the smoke as a powerful genie who has come to do your bidding. You might even see a figure form in the smoke.
3. State your three wishes aloud as affirmations. In your mind's eye, see them coming true. Spend a few minutes focusing on your requests as you inhale the scent of the incense. When you're ready, open the circle.

Ritual 🜍 Clear the Air

An argument or upsetting experience has left bad vibes in your living space. To rid your home of disruptive energy, perform this cleansing ritual.

WHAT YOU NEED

* A broom
* A bowl
* Water
* Sea salt
* Sage (bundled, loose, or incense)

* A fireproof holder that you can carry easily
* Matches or a lighter

BEST TIME TO PERFORM THE SPELL

Any time

WHAT TO DO

1. If possible, open the windows and doors. Start sweeping your home with a broom—not just the floor, but the air as well. Wave the broom through the entire area, side to side, up and down, until you feel you've whisked away the emotional "dirt."

2. Next, fill a bowl with water and add a pinch of sea salt. Sprinkle a little in each corner of your home, then flick some water in the center of each room.

3. Finally, put the sage into the holder and light it. Blow out the flames and let it smoke. Carry the burning sage from room to room, allowing its cleansing smoke to clear the air and restore peace to your home.

Spell ✺ Avoid Bad Traffic

In this spell, the eagle's ability to fly high in the sky symbolizes freedom, and its keen vision signifies being able to see beyond obstacles. Make your drive a little easier with this simple spell that lets the eagle act as your guide.

WHAT YOU NEED

* Scissors
* A sheet of blue construction paper
* A picture of an eagle
* Glue or tape
* A black marker

BEST TIME TO PERFORM THE SPELL

On Wednesday, preferably when the sun and/or moon is in Gemini or Sagittarius

WHAT TO DO

1. Cast a circle around the area where you will do your spell. Use your scissors to cut a circle about 3 inches in diameter from the blue paper. Glue or tape the picture of the eagle in the center.

2. Next, draw the rune *Ehwaz* four times on the paper—at the top, bottom, left, and right of the eagle—to indicate the four directions. *Ehwaz* looks like a capital M and represents movement.

3. Open the circle. Affix the blue paper circle to the dashboard of your car. Each day, before you drive off, spend a few moments focusing your attention on your eagle guide. If you hit heavy traffic or other problems on the road, touch the eagle and ask for its assistance.

Spell ❦ Find the Perfect Parking Spot

Use this spell on those days when it seems like every good spot in the parking lot is taken. Ask the parking goddess Barbara to come to your aid!

WHAT YOU NEED
★ **Nothing but yourself**

BEST TIME TO PERFORM THE SPELL
Any time

WHAT TO DO
1. Stop driving around in circles, close your eyes, and take a few slow, deep breaths. In your mind's eye, see an empty space waiting for you exactly where you want to park. Recite this incantation aloud:
   "Goddess Barbara, fair of face
   Guide me to my parking place."
2. Open your eyes and drive to the spot the goddess has provided for you.

Spell ❦ End Shopping Line Woes

Does it seem that you always manage to get in the slowest line at the supermarket or while out shopping, especially when you're in a hurry? Let Sheila the shopping goddess put you in the fast lane!

WHAT YOU NEED

★ **Nothing but yourself**

BEST TIME TO PERFORM THE SPELL

Any time

WHAT TO DO

1. To make this spell succeed, you have to use your intuition—not logic. As you approach the checkout area of the store, close your eyes, clear your mind, and take a deep breath. Think or quietly say this incantation:
   "Goddess Sheila so divine
   Guide me to the fastest line."

2. Open your eyes. Allow yourself to be drawn to a particular line. Don't analyze it or second guess yourself. The shortest line may not be the fastest, and the shoppers with the fewest number of items in their carts might be the very people who'll dawdle. Trust your instincts.

Incantation 𝐅𝐎𝐑 No Worries

We've all got troubles on our minds, but worrying never makes things better. This spell uses the power of sound plus intention to chase fearful thoughts away and raise positive energy.

WHAT YOU NEED

★ **1 dark blue candle**
★ **1 candleholder**
★ **Matches or a lighter**

★ **A hand drum or gong**
★ **An athame or wand**
★ **A bell**

BEST TIME TO PERFORM THE SPELL
At midnight during the waning moon

WHAT TO DO

1. Cast a circle around the area where you will do your spell. Fit the candle in its holder, set it on your altar (or other surface where it can burn safely), and light it. Begin playing the drum or gong to break up negative thoughts and vibrations. Feel the sound resonating through you, too, stirring up your power and confidence. When you feel ready, chant the following incantation aloud. If possible, shout it out—really assert yourself!

"Doubt and fear
Don't come near.
By the dawn
Be you gone.
By this sign [with your athame or wand draw a
*   pentagram in the air in front of you]*
And light divine
Peace is mine.
I am strong
All day long.
My worries flee
Magickally.
I ring this bell [ring the bell]
To bind this spell,
And all is well."

2. As you chant, envision your fears receding into the darkness, losing their strength. When you're ready, extinguish the candle and open the circle.

Spell ᶠᵒᴿ Extra Strength

A daunting challenge looms before you. Call in some extra muscle. Since ancient times, the people of India have drawn upon the strength of the elephant god Ganesh to help them overcome seemingly insurmountable obstacles. So can you.

WHAT YOU NEED

★ **An athame (or kitchen knife)**

BEST TIME TO PERFORM THE SPELL

On a Saturday, or when the sun and/or moon is in Capricorn

WHAT TO DO

1. Cast a circle around the area where you will do your spell. Close your eyes and imagine you're in a dark, dense jungle. The vegetation is so thick you can see only a foot or two ahead of you. Dangers lurk unseen. You feel trapped and helpless. The tangled vines and thick overgrowth represent the obstacles facing you.

2. Suddenly you hear the trumpeting call of an elephant— it's Ganesh coming to your rescue. Pick up your athame (or kitchen knife). Without hesitation, he rushes toward you and easily lifts you with his trunk onto his back.

3. Explain to him the nature of your problem. Visualize yourself riding on Ganesh's back as he marches into the jungle, trampling everything in his path.

4. Reach out with your athame and begin slashing away at the vines and branches, hacking through the obstacles. See space opening up before you. Feel Ganesh's strength, lifting you high above your problems. Together you are unstoppable. Keep chopping away at the thick vegetation, eliminating obstacles one by one. When you feel ready, climb down from Ganesh's back and thank him for his assistance. Open the circle. Repeat as necessary.

Spell FOR a "Knotty" Situation

A stressful situation has you all tied up in knots. This spell uses the symbolism of knots to help you get out the kinks and release tension.

WHAT YOU NEED

★ A piece of nonsynthetic cord or rope as long as your spine
★ Matches or a lighter

BEST TIME TO PERFORM THE SPELL
During the waning moon

WHAT TO DO

1. Choose a piece of cord or rope in a color that represents your dilemma: green for money woes, pink for troubles in love, and so on. Cast a circle around the area where you will do your spell. Tie several knots in the rope to represent difficulties. These signify the areas where you feel bound by problems.

2. When you're ready, slowly untie one knot. Envision the tension in the situation easing as you loosen the knot. Feel your mind begin to relax and let go of the problem. Untie another knot and visualize another blockage being removed. See or sense your heart and mind opening up, becoming more receptive and less rigid.

3. Keep untying the knots one at a time. Don't hurry; work at your own pace. With each knot, a problem or a part of the overall problem is resolved.

4. As you continue you may receive ideas about how to handle the difficulties represented by the knots or gain deeper insight into your own role in the problem. When you've finished untying all the knots, breathe a sigh of relief and let yourself feel calm, confident, and untroubled. Open the circle and burn the rope.

Early Morning Divination FOR Advice

You're facing down a tough challenge and you don't know where to turn for advice. If only the universe would give you a sign! Long ago Celtic prognosticators known as frithir read the signs of the times from the first thing that caught their attention when they stepped outside. Try this ancient divination technique to get the guidance you need.

WHAT YOU NEED
★ Nothing but yourself

BEST TIME TO PERFORM THE SPELL
The first Monday after a solstice or equinox

WHAT TO DO
1. Immediately after arising in the morning—before you do anything else—sit quietly for a few minutes and contemplate the situation that has you in a quandary.
2. Go to your door and close your eyes. Take three slow, deep breaths before opening the door.
3. Open the door and step outside, if you can do this safely with your eyes closed. Otherwise just stand in the open doorway facing out. Open your eyes. What's the first thing you see? What significance does it hold for you? A squirrel could suggest that you get busy gathering money, information, or other resources. A butterfly might mean a change is coming.

4. Notice any impressions or feelings that arise into your awareness—they may be significant. If you don't sense an immediate answer, simply tuck away the memory of what you've seen and allow it to percolate in your subconscious. You might want to do some research into classic symbolism associated with the object that caught your attention. Pretty soon, perhaps in a dream, you'll receive the guidance you've been seeking.

Manifesting Your Dreams

A particular wish probably won't materialize overnight; it's going to take a while to develop. While you're waiting, cast this spell to nurture your dreams and help make them a reality.

WHAT YOU NEED

- ★ A sheet of paper
- ★ Scissors
- ★ A pen or pencil
- ★ A cauldron (or other bowl-shaped container)
- ★ Powdered ginger
- ★ Blessed thistle (dried herb, capsules, or tablets)
- ★ A green cloth

BEST TIME TO PERFORM THE SPELL

The day after the new moon

WHAT TO DO

1. Cast a circle around the area where you will do your spell. Cut the sheet of paper into twelve strips. On one strip write your wish in the form of an affirmation. Fold the paper strip three times and put it in the cauldron. Sprinkle a little powdered ginger in the cauldron (to speed up results) and a little blessed thistle (to help your goal manifest) by simply opening a capsule or grinding a tablet into powder, then adding it to the cauldron. Cover the cauldron with the green cloth. Open the circle.

2. Allow the spell to "simmer" overnight. In the morning remove the cloth and repeat the spell. Continue in this manner for a total of twelve days. If your wish hasn't materialized by the time of the full moon, take a break during the waning moon period and begin again on the first day of the waxing moon. Don't give up—trust that your wish will manifest when the time is right.

Spell to Get Rid of Old Baggage

Are old habits, fears, and outdated attitudes getting in the way of your success? This spell helps you eliminate old baggage so it doesn't keep weighing you down.

WHAT YOU NEED

* A piece of paper
* A pen or pencil
* Matches or a lighter
* A cauldron or other fireproof container

BEST TIME TO PERFORM THE SPELL

During the waning moon

WHAT TO DO

1. Cast a circle around the area where you will do your spell. On the paper, write down whatever it is you want to eliminate from your life. Describe how this old baggage is limiting you. If you like, explore what you believe to be the root of the condition. Allow your emotions to come up and write about how you feel.

2. When you've finished, read what you've written. Then crumple the paper loosely, light it, and drop it in the cauldron. As the paper burns, envision your old baggage burning up too. When the paper has completely burned, allow the ashes to cool. Open the circle.

3. Take the ashes to a cemetery. Say aloud: "This old part of my life is dead and gone, and I am now free of its influence." Scatter the ashes in the wind.

Spell FOR a Step in the Right Direction

A lighthearted approach is sometimes best when dealing with everyday troubles. Don't be put off by the playful quality of the spell—it can be quite powerful.

WHAT YOU NEED

★ Nail polish
★ Polish remover
★ Cotton balls and/or swabs

BEST TIME TO PERFORM THE SPELL

Depends on your intentions (see Chapter 5)

WHAT TO DO

1. Select one or more bottles of nail polish, in colors that correspond to your intentions: pink or red for love, green or gold for money, and so on. Cast a circle around the area where you will do your spell.

2. Assign an objective to each toe. You can give all ten toes the same intention or pick ten different goals—or any other combination. Begin painting your toenails in colors that are appropriate to your objectives.

3. As you paint each nail, concentrate on your intention and envision it already manifesting. If you like, decorate your nails with symbols that represent your intentions: dollar signs for money, hearts for love, and so on.

4. Have fun and be creative. If you change your mind, simply remove the polish and start over.

5. Allow the polish to dry, then open the circle. For as long as the polish lasts, each step you take will bring you closer to your goals.

Spell ⟞ Send Wishes to the Universe

What do you wish for? A new car? A better job? Money to take a dream vacation? The sky's the limit! This high-flying spell sends your requests far and wide so the universe can fulfill your heart's desires.

WHAT YOU NEED

* ★ A kite
* ★ Ribbons of different colors
* ★ A pen that will write on fabric

BEST TIME TO PERFORM THE SPELL

Depends on your intentions (see Chapter 5)

WHAT TO DO

1. Select ribbons of colors that correspond to your desires: pink for love, gold for money, and so on. Cast a circle around the area where you will do your spell.

2. On each ribbon, write one wish. Remember to state your request in the form of an affirmation. Attach the ribbons to a kite. Visualize your wishes coming true. When you're finished, open the circle.

3. Take the kite outside to an open area without interference. As you watch the kite soaring in the sky, imagine the wind catching your requests and carrying them to the four corners of the earth. Have fun—a positive attitude will help your intentions manifest faster.

Charm FOR Good Luck

Would you like to help your friends and loved ones with their problems by boosting their good luck throughout the coming year? This Yuletide custom lets you make a unique magickal gift for everyone on your list.

WHAT YOU NEED

- ★ A Yule log (usually oak)
- ★ Matches or a lighter
- ★ A cloth drawstring pouch for each friend/ loved one on your gift list
- ★ Dried pink rose petals (for love)
- ★ Dried lavender buds or leaves (for peace of mind)
- ★ Dried basil (for protection)
- ★ Dried mint leaves (for prosperity)
- ★ Dried echinacea (for health)
- ★ A sheet of paper
- ★ Scissors
- ★ A pen

BEST TIME TO PERFORM THE SPELL

Yule (usually December 21)

WHAT TO DO

1. On the night of the Winter Solstice, build a Yule fire in a safe place and burn an oak log in it. Allow the fire to burn down completely. The next morning when the ashes have cooled, scoop some into each pouch. Add the dried botanicals.

2. Cut the sheet of paper into slips, one for each person on your list. Write a personalized wish on each slip of paper. Fold the papers three times and add them to the pouches. Tie the pouches closed and give them to your loved ones.

Index